BREAKING

UNGODLY SOUL TIES

By

MICHAEL PITTS

BREAKING

UNGODLY SOUL TIES

by Michael Pitts

M.A.P.S. Institute
Swanton, Ohio

Breaking Ungodly Soul Ties
Published by:
M.A.P.S. Institute
Swanton, OH 43603
U.S.A.

Editorial Consultant: Denyse Cummings, North Little Rock, AR

Art Direction: Marcia K. Culp

cover Design by: Bryant Design Group, 9838 Old Baymeadows Road, Suite 377, Jacksonville, FL 32256
cover illustration is protected by the 1976 United States Copyright Act.
Copyright © 1997 by M.A.P.S. Institute

Book Production by: Dickinson Press, 5100 33rd Street SE, Grand Rapids, MI 49512

For Speaking engagements, you may contact the author at:

CORNERSTONE CHURCH
P.O.Box 351690
Toledo, OH 43635
Website:
www.cornerstonechurch.us

ISBN # 0-9726718-0-3

Printed in the United States of America.

BREAKING UNGODLY SOUL TIES...
Assisting God's people in breaking free from every bondage and shaking off snares, delusions and hinderances of their souls.

-Michael Pitts

CONTENTS

Also by
Michael Pitts

Breaking the Assignment of Spiritual Assassins

A Dictionary Of Contemporary Christian Words And Concepts

Don't Curse Your Crisis

Help! I Think God Is Trying To Kill Me

Living on The Edge

Making The Holy Spirit Your Partner

INTRODUCTION

TAKE OFF THE MASK

God is in the process of teaching His people how to untangle their lives. It's true that the "world" is walking in deception, desolation and death. But God has not directed me to write this book about the problems of the world.

I have been directed to address the people of God; the ones who have been eternally justified, sanctified, redeemed, and cleansed with the very Life of God — but continue to walk as the world walks — depressed, confused, and irrational.

I want the people of God to break free from every bondage and to shake off the snares, delusions, and hindrances of their souls. Ungodly soul ties have suppressed the destinies, and the eternal purposes of God, frustrating plans for many individuals. These believers are wearing spiritual masks; and hiding behind it are real pains, heartaches, and soulish discouragement.

I realize that there are psychological and social truths concerning the factors of an ungodly soul tie. But I'm not writing this book by either one of those standards. I believe that I am anointed by God to bring you the spiritual focus and truths of an ungodly soul tie, and thereby destroy its devastating and disillusioning effects on your life.

Until I began to ask the Lord questions about a soul tie, I always wondered why people would come to the altar and accept Jesus Christ as their Savior and then fail to continue with Him. I witnessed, as undoubtedly you have, many believers who would rise to a certain level only to fall and miss the mark. You may, while reading this book, be able to identify people who are struggling with soul ties and God will use you to set them free.

I'm going to speak very plainly in this book; because it takes accuracy to break an ungodly soul tie. You may read some things that make you nervous and uncomfortable; but if you'll keep reading, you'll find freedom. Jesus is not committed to how comfortable you can be; but He is committed to your freedom.

I want you to commit to reading every page of this book. Don't skip around to the sections that you *think* you need. You need all of it, or you would not be reading it. I believe that a great deliverance is coming into your life. My friend, the peace of God is just ahead.

Right now before we go any further, I want you to make a decision to lower your guard and allow the Holy Spirit to deal with you in an intense, internal honesty. If you will, I believe, in the Name of Jesus, that godly insight, understanding, and freedom will be yours by the end of this book!

Chapter 1

"GOD, WHAT *IS* AN UNGODLY SOUL TIE?"

A few years ago, I began to study a pattern in Christian living. I would watch as strong and eager believers would come into the church, carrying their Bibles and worshipping the Lord. Their faces would shine with the glory of God, and the anointing of increase was upon their lives.

But in a matter of months, something began to change with them. These same believers began to act irrational, strange, and secretive. Sometimes they would even begin to talk or dress differently. They began to carry themselves differently. They seemed to have lost their focus on God. As I watched them, they seemed either to be a million miles away, or they were conscious of what everyone else was doing. I noticed that their godly exuberance had turned more into "coping" than "commitment."

At first, I put them all into one category. I thought the way most of us do, when we fail to give each situation our individual attention. I chalked them up as "out of the Word" or "backslidden" in some area.

However, I couldn't help but notice that most of these people never missed a church service or gathering. Many of these people knew about demonic strongholds and were skilled in spiritual warfare. They knew about the Blood of Jesus, the righteousness He purchased for us, and the free gift of grace by the power of the Holy Spirit.

It was just that their behavior had turned lethargic and their faces seemed plastic and confused. They were just "going through the motions."

Now, this behavior didn't just happen to new believers. It also happened to people that had known God for years. I even saw people in the ministry who were affected by it! It didn't seem to matter if the believer was immature or mature, or if they had been born again for a month or a decade. It seemed that this behavior came out of nowhere and no one was immune.

Some of them did fall away from the church and from God. Their entire lifestyles changed dramatically. The things they once gave their lives for now meant nothing to them. Their peace was gone, their marriages were torn apart, and their health was depleted. In short, their lives were in shambles.

Some of these people would come to the altar for me to pray for them. As I laid my hands on them, I noticed a divine urgency rising up from within me. Each time, a commandment would come up out of my spirit and I would say, "I break the ungodly soul tie."

I didn't know what I was saying, but I continued to respond to my spirit and pray for the people, seeing visible results. After experiencing this divine direction several times I finally asked the Lord, "What is this I'm saying? What is an ungodly soul tie?"

THREE DANGERS OF OUR GENERATION

Before I begin to break down the aspects of an ungodly soul tie, I want to lay a foundational summary of the way this generation thinks and operates today. In order for you to see why an ungodly soul tie is so detrimental, you must first understand the delusions that society is constantly presenting to you. If you don't know any better, you'll be pulled into their snare without even realizing it.

Now, an ungodly soul tie is **when the emotions, the mind, and the will of a person becomes entangled to the point where their thoughts are no longer their own**. In other words, the ungodly soul tie occurs when **a person is unnaturally and inordinately affected by the will, the emotions, and the desires of another person**.

In the following chapters, we're going to thoroughly explore the behaviors of an ungodly soul tie, and the situations in which an ungodly soul tie begins. We will discuss both the humorous and the devastating situations that point to the ungodly soul tie. We are also going to discuss the various attributes of a godly covenant and an ungodly covenant.

But first, it's very important that we look at some areas that plague our generation as a whole. Repeatedly I have noticed that our nation thrives on stimulation. The more stimulated we can be, the more interested we will be. Our generation uses several areas to excessively stimulate their minds in order to fill the voids in their lives.

What is the number one reason that people become involved in an ungodly soul tie? They lose their focus. How do people lose their focus? They try to live more than one lifestyle.

If God is your main focus, you'll only live one way. However, if you become divided, or if any of these three generational obsessions become your dominant focus, you could fall as a victim to an ungodly soul tie.

1: THE HUNGER FOR INFORMATION

Number one, our generation is made up of *information-seeking* people. The American public is extremely inquisitive. It doesn't matter what the subject is, our generation wants to hear from everyone that knows anything about it. Years ago, if a physician told you that you needed surgery, the procedure was understood and scheduled. Today, we get three other medical opinions, read various articles, watch medical videos, and seek advice from talk shows before we make the final decision.

If you are not careful, you will bring that abuse into the church. You'll read and feed on the opinions of various speakers and various outlooks until you think you can pick and choose *how* you want to believe about something. The Bible has sound, proven answers to each question. It is up to us to find it and follow it.

I'm not against information. But I am warning against the abuse of "opinionated information" and slanted journalism because it leads to confusion. Not everything you read is true. In this generation, it is imperative that we operate from our spirits to discern the truth from the lie.

A governmental church is designed by God to empower you by presenting to you scriptural information and nurturing spiritual growth, that you may victoriously navigate the treacherous waters of life. The leader that is called by God will make sure that you have all the sound doctrine and godly correction you can handle to be able to live life successfully. Authoritative, apostolic leaders understand today's current events in a relevant, biblical perspective and they won't water down the truth with flimsy, slanted opinions or a "do-your-own-thing" outlook.

The delusions and deceptions of this generation have done many things to keep the multitudes from trusting in the counsel of the Church. Giving heed and credibility to all opinions presented to them, our culture has reduced the scriptures and the voices of godly leaders to the level of popular faddish personalities, who themselves are void of legitimate authority. But in spite of the lies of men, you still have a choice — to believe God's Word or man's. Here's what Second Chronicles, chapter twenty, verse twenty says:

"...Believe in the Lord your God, so shall ye be established; believe his prophets, so shall ye prosper."

The government of God — the Church — and its appointed representatives are the only sources on earth that are anointed for increase. It's not the tabloids, the liberated magazines, the political newspapers, or the business journals. God's called and anointed men and women will be the ones to keep you established, keep you free and keep you prospering.

#2: THE HUNGER FOR SPIRITUALITY

Secondly, America is searching for spiritual answers. It is wrong to say that we are a nation of unbelief. Instead, our problem is that we believe *everything* — New Age, reincarnation, eastern religions, native religions, crystals, meditation and so on.

It's a documented fact that the Psychic Network has the highest profit of all the 900 numbers. Even scanning your television channels, you can't miss their commercials. Have you ever noticed the network is hosted by scores of actors and actresses who are out of work or who are very low on the popularity scale? That in itself should give you a clue of their "psychic" direction.

The Church is where spirituality should be evident and the answers clear. Instead, the devil has deceived the Church into thinking that the world will not come if we act spiritual. It seems the Church has reasoned that the world will stay away unless they make their services "comfortable" for them. So, the Church has been guilty of watering down the services, perverting their authority, quenching the Spirit, or shortening their messages to appease the flesh.

The Church wants to please the world and the world wants the spiritual. Everything is backwards. However, I believe the situation is about to be divinely reversed.

21

You have a covenant with God to follow Him and know His Word. That agreement with God is not bondage — it's a covenant of freedom and protection. If you allow yourself to be seduced by any other spiritual perceptions, you will find yourself entangled in an ungodly soul tie.

#3: THE HUNGER FOR RELATIONSHIPS

Lastly, the American public is desperately searching for relationships. We are a relationship-oriented society. If you do not believe that, just look at the magazine covers the next time you stand in line at the grocery store. The headlines scream, "Four Ways To Please Your Man," or "Ten Secrets That Women Wish Men Knew," and so on.

Soap operas, the number one day-time shows, wouldn't have a script if it weren't for goofy, roller-coaster relationships. There are daily talk shows based totally on freak relationships and "dating columns" in the national newspapers. Psychologists are booked solid for three weeks counseling those with broken relationships. And if you looked hard enough, you would find that most drug addiction and alcohol abuse in our nation come from the hurts in relationships.

Well, the Church is a place where relationships should come forth and flourish. It is a setting where there is security in fellowship and friendships. It's a place where marriages can stabilize and mature. It is an environment where we should all be pressing toward the same revelations, motivations, and goals. The Church is designed to be an environment for relationships that are both successful and fun. Unfortunately, it's also a place where ungodly soul ties attempt to enter, devastate, and destroy.

Chapter 2

LET'S TALK ABOUT "REAL" FREEDOM

Freedom is a process. It's not always immediate. Works of the flesh will always produce frustrations, confusion and entanglements. Sometimes, it takes some time to untangle our situations. But the grace of God — which is the power of God — will always come when we are obedient to His Word.

Legally, we are free at the point of salvation. Experientially, we taste personal freedom level after level. In the book of Deuteronomy, the Israelites destroyed their enemies little by little as they obeyed God. In the New Testament, we are to go from glory to glory as we follow and obey God, and become saturated with His presence.

But you can only experience a new level of freedom when you've had enough of the old level. One day you will say, "I refuse to be a failure any longer. I refuse to be depressed any longer," and refuse to lose the same battle again. Then you'll begin to experience a new level of freedom. The light of God will begin to shine in your life and you'll see a pattern that has soulishly assaulted you, working in your family, in your generation, and many in our nation. When you proclaim "I'm going to put a stop to this," what was *legally* true at your spiritual birth becomes *experientially* true in your natural surroundings.

IS YOUR HOUSE IN ORDER?

Let's look at Third John, verse two.

"Beloved, I wish above all things that thou mayest prosper and be in health, even as thy soul prospereth."

God wants you to experience new levels in Him. But there is a condition. The condition is in this verse: "Even as" or commensurate to, your **soul** prospering.

The picture you see on the back of this book is not all there is to Michael Pitts. This picture shows one part of me, but I have three parts to my being — and so do you. Man is a spirit, he has a soul and he lives in a body. So we could say that man is a house with three rooms. Our spirit is saved at the point of salvation. Our soul is in the process of being saved while we live. And our body shall be saved at the Second Coming of the Lord Jesus Christ.

While on earth, man is designed to live in relationship with God through his spirit, through his soul and through his body. When a man's body is in relationship with God, he is *healthy*. When his soul is in relationship with God, he is *happy*. When his spirit is in relationship with God, he is *holy*. When all three parts are functioning totally in harmony with Him, there is righteousness, peace and joy.

God wants your entire "house" serving Him as one. Why? Because a house divided against itself cannot stand. We must understand that the inheritance of our salvation covers every area of our lives. Salvation is in the past, present, and future tense. It's salvation for the mind, the body, and relationships. It is salvation from demonic assault. It is total and complete.

Our inheritance makes an open and inviting provision for prosperity of the soul realm. Each part of man is a whole realm of its own to be explored and enjoyed. But in this book, we are primarily dealing with the realm of the soul.

LIVING FROM THE INSIDE OUT

The soul realm of man consists of his emotions, his mind, his will, and his intellect. Most of the battles we face in life are really fought in the soulical realm.

Remember, the spirit is already saved and in constant communion with God. But the soulical realm — our minds, our thoughts, our memories, our emotions, our wills, our desires — are always under satanic attack. Those areas are constantly in the balance of decision. That's why the soul is being saved and renewed daily through the written and spoken Word of the Lord.

If the enemy can gain control over your will, if he can gain control over your "want-to," over your memories, over your thoughts, then he will begin to manipulate your life and body to live at a level far below the destiny God has prepared for you.

So, according to Third John, verse two, your thoughts, memories, will, and intellect must be healthy and godly in order for you to fully prosper in every area of life. According to the Word of God, prosperity works its way from the inside out. When you prosper on the inside, something begins to happen on the outside.

Too many times we look for an outward manifestation when there has been no inward change. Remember, the life for God is lived from the inside out.

What do I mean by that? It's simple. You cannot live your life according to circumstances. Circumstances seldom present an optimistic view of your future. You can't wake up in the morning and wonder how you're going to live. You cannot look at your life pessimistically and see what it has handed you to decide how you are going to live. You have to decide on the inside, "I will live the way

God wants me to live." Then you take that fortitude and begin to attack the trials of life with a pre-determined plan for victory.

Understand that you determine how your life will go today. Oh yes, plans will be interrupted and changes will always come. But you are the one who alters your attitude to prevail over them. It takes faith to believe God and open the channel for Him to perform His will through you in the earth.

Kathryn Kuhlman had a great saying about life. She said, "If you don't know what you are going to do with life, then life will find something to do with you." So you cannot ask life, "What will I do? What will I be?" You do not base your future on what others have been before you, or what your family has done, or what society expects you to be. You cannot be less than what your race, culture, gender or education has allowed you to be. No! You start on the inside and ask, "God, what do You want me to be?" Then everything else has to get out of the way, because, if you prosper on the inside, you will have prosperity on the outside!

After you have made that decision, there will be attributes that follow the prosperous soul. Let's discuss a few of those signs.

Chapter 3

THE PROSPEROUS SOUL

One of the greatest attributes of a prosperous soul is *self-authority*.

God has given you authority over yourself. That means your life is not determined by circumstances. It's not determined by what others think of you. You are designed to be in charge of yourself.

When you realize that you've been given self-authority, your emotional well-being is not in the hands of other people. When your soul is prosperous, no one can make you be what you don't want to be. The expectations of another do not determine how you will react to life's events. No one can make you mad because you are in charge of your soul. No one can drive you crazy because you've taken the keys out of their hands.

When I speak of self-authority, I am not talking about rebellion. I'm talking about the self-authority that produces reliability.

Reliability is the ability to make a decision and follow through with it. You can say to someone, "I will meet you at one o'clock at such and such place," then lo and behold, at one o'clock, you are there. Self-authority produces reliability.

We all know people who will tell you, "I'm going to

meet you tomorrow at such and such time and place," and we all know while they are yet speaking that they won't be there. They will however, have a list of excuses and reasons.

The road to ruin is filled with people that had good intentions. But the real issue is that they were not in charge of themselves. When you are prosperous in your soul, you have the ability to make a decision and stick to it.

The next sign of self-authority is the ability to react to life's situations in a realistic manner.

If you are not in charge of yourself, any little thing can set you off. However, if you are in control of your soul, a temporary problem will not cause you to react in a drastic manner.

Let's use an example that we can all relate to. You are driving down the road and suddenly your car breaks down. What do you do? Some become so angry that they jump out of the car and pound it, kick it, or curse it. They act like the car had purposely done something to them! At one time or another, I'm sure we've all thought about beating our car for the humiliation and injustice that it has thrust upon us. But be realistic here. Your car is not against you and has no plans to humiliate you. It is not upset with you and has not chosen to break down on your important day.

Your car is not a living thing; it's simply a vehicle. It's foolish to try and reason with something that can't respond. Handle the situation in a realistic manner and complete your day.

Or, maybe you are behind on your bills and suddenly, you receive another unexpected bill. People who do not know how to react in a realistic manner may either go into a deep depression, or they overreact in anger and punch a hole in the wall. Now you've created yet another bill!

Instead of foolishly reacting to the situation, devise a strategy. Call your creditors and work out a payment plan that you can live with. It's foolish to react drastically to a temporary problem.

The next sign of a prosperous soul is the ability to relate to a variety of people.

If the only people you can get along with are folks that are like you in upbringing, race, or economic bracket, then you're in trouble. Jesus was so big on the inside that He could easily relate to anyone. He could relate to a variety of people without therapy, nerve pills or talk show hosts. Why? Because Jesus was prosperous in His soul, and He is our great example.

Although God enjoys and protects heritage and culture, the Gospel itself is not cultural. The hand of God *and* move of God have never come from or been based upon a particular culture or skin color. The participation in the move of God is based upon the heart of man, not the color of man.

Those with racial prejudices have attempted to divert and pervert the Gospel. It seems they have formed their own classifications of the human race, then divided mankind into certain groups — black, white, red, yellow, poor, rich, good, bad. But the Bible has only two classifications — dead or alive. Believer or unbeliever. Scripturally, a person is either dead to Christ or alive in Him, and that should be our only standard as well.

The more oppressed a person becomes in their soul, the more they lose their ability to relate to someone of another color or culture. These types of people soon form a perverted soul tie to their own race, believing other races to be inferior and treacherous. Oppression has a narrow, segmented view. Depending upon the degree of oppression, one of two things will result — either you will

29

become a critical racist or cower as an isolated hermit.

Have you ever noticed that the more oppressed you become in your soul, the fewer people you want to be around? If you don't get help, pretty soon you won't want to be around people at all. To you, the word "people" will mean "trouble" and "aggravation." You'll want to move someplace high in the mountains where we can only get to you by plane. Or, you'll be found sitting in a dark, cluttered house with fifty cats.

Jesus never intended for you to be an island or a commune. He created you to have a prosperous soul so that you can be a light to the people of the world. As soon as you rid yourself of the oppression that's holding you, you'll see it. The world needs you. That's why He gave you a body to be here. You have a purpose and a destiny and **it will always** involve the people of the world.

Another important sign of self-authority is the ability to respond properly to godly authority without feeling threatened.

There will always be authority. God established different kinds of authority in every sphere of life. There is authority in government, in cities, in schools, on the job, in the home, and in the Church. God designed authority to lead you into success.

When people have a problem all through their life with authority, it is because there's something wrong on the inside of them. Those that fight authority are insecure and confused. They're disturbed with their own lives, so they voice that inner disturbance through rebellion. Their own soul is in turmoil, so they react in jealousy, rage or deceit against those who have a plan in life. The fight against authority is a sign that a soul is not prospering.

On the other hand, a prosperous soul realizes that every person has a different place and a different measure of authority. If someone is in authority over you in one place, it does not make them smarter, more spiritual, or of greater value to God. It simply means that everyone must fulfill their function. A prosperous soul knows who they are and where they are going, so they are able to respond to authority without feeling smaller themselves.

Chapter 4

NOT "WHAT," BUT "WHO?"

We've laid some important foundations on the atmosphere of our nation, the three parts of man, and the prosperous soul. By gaining a clearer understanding along these lines, we are now ready to analyze the ungodly soul tie and its devastating effects on an individual.

First of all, not all relationships have an ungodly soul tie. The ungodly soul tie is a counterfeit for the godly covenant. In a godly covenant your soul is naturally involved, but there is a great amount of individuality, peace and freedom to be the person God created you to be. Your soul must be *involved* in a good relationship; but it was never meant for your soul to be *tied* to or controlled by a relationship.

Here's the difference. Remember the definition: An ungodly soul tie is when **the emotions, the mind, and the will of more than one person become intertwined to the place where the thoughts of the individual are no longer their own**. In other words, **they are unnaturally and inordinately affected by the will, the emotions, and the desires of another person**.

If everything you think about, everything you relate to, every place you go, everything you say, and every way you dress is based upon another person, your soul is more than involved. Your soul is tied. You've lost your individuality and that makes your responses ungodly. The ungodly soul tie is in direct opposition to the way God intended for your soul to be involved in a relationship.

"WHO" HAS BEWITCHED YOU?

For scriptural insight, let's look at Galatians 3:1.

"O foolish Galatians, who hath bewitched you, that ye should not obey the truth, before whose eyes Jesus Christ hath been evidently set forth, crucified among you?"

Now read what the *Amplified Version* of Galatians 3:1 says:

"O you poor and silly and thoughtless and unreflecting and senseless Galatians! Who has fascinated or bewitched or cast a spell over you, unto whom — right before your very eyes — Jesus Christ (the Messiah) was openly and graphically set forth and portrayed as crucified?"

Notice that neither version says, *"What"* has bewitched or put a spell on you. Instead these scriptures directly pinpoint the source of the problem — *"Who"* has put a spell on you? Understand this and hear me well. The bewitching, the soul tie, the spell is not the result of a circumstance. It is not the result of outside stimuli. **It is the result of a person**.

Someone doesn't have to come into your house in a grass skirt with a bag of bones to put a spell on you. The Bible teaches us through these scriptures that when someone knows the truth but will not obey it, the question we need to ask is not *"What* has happened to you?" but *"Who* are you talking to?"

WHO ARE YOU, ANYWAY?

There are many people who act a certain way in one crowd and yet, when they get with a particular person they lose their individual identity. Suddenly, while in the presence of that other person, their own thoughts and actions are no longer their own. Why? Because they've been tied up in the soul realm. They have an ungodly soul tie to that other person and as a result, are unrighteously influenced by them.

Why do I define that kind of behavior as unrighteous? Because a person with a righteous mentality knows who he is. That person doesn't lose his identity. He operates from a spirit in control over circumstances. Anytime you are with another person and you lose your individuality; whenever your thoughts cease to be your own or you're concerned about saying the right things to please that person, you are allowing yourself to be unrighteously influenced. It's an ungodly soul tie.

When someone knows the truth but does not want to do it, the devil will be sure to send someone their way to offer a rationale as to why that word no longer applies. When you choose their word over the Spirit of Life, you become out of order. Your body and your soul no longer follow the leading of your spirit. Instead you've now placed your soul on the throne, your body follows it and your spirit is silenced. Whatever has led you out of balance will always come to the top. And whatever is on the top will be the source where all decisions are made. In the ungodly soul tie, it is the soul that is out of balance and on the top. As a result, everything has to serve the wants, the desires and the reasoning of a needy soul.

Certainly you can see that by placing the soul over the leading of the spirit, the relationship will always come to a negative, sometimes disastrous conclusion. It doesn't matter how bad you want the relationship or what you are soulishly willing to do to keep it. It doesn't matter if you both have positions within a church. It doesn't matter if you have an endless supply of financial prosperity. The results are always the same, no matter your mindset, your position, or your personal status. There are no exceptions. Why? Because the ungodly soul tie is a counterfeit for a godly covenant. The unrighteous, ungodly soul tie will never produce godly results; it will only lead to destruction, dysfunction, and ruin.

Chapter 5

THE GODLY COVENANT

Before we go further with revealing the ungodly soul tie, I want to lay a the foundation in order to define a godly covenant, or godly relationship.

Some of you reading this book have never been involved in a godly relationship. It's very important for you to see the difference between the godly covenant and the ungodly counterfeit. By understanding the differences and branding these truths on your heart, you will always be able to know if a relationship is in the will of God.

The number one requirement in a godly relationship is that the other person in your life is committed to your spiritual growth.

Now, by spiritual growth, I'm talking about God, His Spirit, and His Word — not yoga, New Age, crystals, astrology, reincarnation, or meditation. If your best friend is not born-again and doesn't want anything to do with serving God, then you are not in a godly relationship. People can change; but if they refuse to be or cannot be committed to the most important thing in your life, which is spiritual growth in God, let them go and pray for them. Then ask God to send the friends you need.

Another point in a godly relationship is that you are not always put in the position of the giver.

A godly relationship is mutually beneficial. If you are in a relationship and you are the only one giving, the only one trying, and you always come in the back end of the deal, then the relationship is not of God. God will not place His approval on a relationship if helping them is hurting you. The relationship that's in a godly covenant gives and receives with joy. It is mutually beneficial, enjoyable, and desirable. Don't come out on the short end of the deal. The saying is true that we are servants to all; but it's also true that we should be slaves to none. Come out of that slump and find God's best for you!

A godly relationship does not cause you to violate your conscience.

If you constantly have to tell your friend that you will not go to a bar or cruise the streets, then something is wrong. If you constantly have to stand against their suggestions to miss church and spend your Sunday mornings going hiking and looking at nature, then face it — something is out of balance in the friendship. In its present condition, it's not a God-ordained relationship. Remember, people can change and turn to God. But if they don't and if you are committed to serving Jesus Christ, just how much could you and your friend have in common?

You can have unbelievers as friends. And, if they have the right respect for their relationship with you, they will not try to persuade you to do something that violates your God-given conscience. However, if you have to re-establish every week that you do not run around on your mate, you don't do this and you don't do that, then it is time for you to sever that relationship.

A godly relationship does not manipulate through anger, but motivates through love.

Have you ever heard someone say, "If I don't do that, so and so is really going to be mad at me?" How horrible it must be to live in a relationship where you're afraid to voice your opinion.

There are many of you reading this book whose personalities have been altered by someone's manipulation. If you do not do what the other person expects, they will have a major fit. Thinking that you cannot handle that, you do what they want - and it continues until you no longer know what *you* want. Guess what? If they have a fit and you're not around, you don't have to deal with it! If someone else wants to live out of their soulish manipulations, let them do it. But whatever you do, keep yourself free from their entanglements. Remember, people with a righteous mentality know who they are and refuse to lose their individuality.

There is a spiritual dynamic, or a spiritual law in the Bible that is referred to as the "law of association." Proverbs 13:20 explains it this way:

> *"He that walketh with wise men shall be wise: but a companion of fools shall be destroyed."*

In other words, your life will rise or fall to the level of your associations. If you want to know where you are going, just take a look at your friends.

Let's look at how the *Amplified Version* interprets I Corinthians 15:33:

> *"Do not be so deceived and misled! Evil companionships (communion, associations) corrupt and deprave good manners and morals and character."*

These verses establish a truth that you will become like those you closely associate with. Bad company, or ungodly relationships, will cause you to fall to the level of your association with them.

A simple example of this truth is seen with children. Let's say your children start running around or playing with the wrong children. Suddenly they come back into your home using words they have never heard in your house, or they take up habits that were never allowed under your roof. As parents, you protected your children and taught them godly principles and behavior. But because they've closely associated with the wrong kind of people, they have turned into another child. Why? Because bad company corrupts good morals.

Understand that when I speak of ungodly soul ties, I'm not just talking about natural mannerisms or behavioral patterns. The ungodly soul tie goes deeper than that. If left unchecked, it turns into a supernatural bewitching that seeks to sear the conscience and pierce the spirit of the person affected. Once the ungodly soul tie is allowed to get to this level, a demonic control takes over. This demonic control creeps in upon the person until he is no longer who he once was. His thoughts and his attitudes cease to be his own. Sadly, this person will wake up some morning and find he is spiritually and soulishly strangled by the control and manipulation of the ungodly soul tie.

Because of this very reason, many of God's people are entangled and bound. They pretend they are free; but in reality, they can no longer run the race for God. No matter how they cover it up, the truth is they now find it hard to live for God. Why? Because they have allowed some other person to bewitch them, or put a spell on them. They're not allowed to feel what God wants them to feel because they are bound up by someone else. Now they cannot even think for themselves without wondering what the other person will say or think about it.

I want you to know it is my prayer that in the Name that is above every name, that every ungodly attack of the devil, and the ungodly soul tie, will be broken off your life and the life of those you love. I am here to proclaim to you that there is freedom and deliverance coming to the people of God! Whatever you do, keep reading and allow the Spirit of God to divinely intervene and change your situation.

Chapter 6

THE UNGODLY COVENANT : SOUL TIES

Many things that have been said have jolted some of you into reality. But, I'm going to go even further. In order to help yourself or someone else, you must have the ability to properly diagnose the problem. Let's talk about the signs that accompany the ungodly soul tie.

BEHAVIORAL SIGN #1:

AN UNGODLY SOUL TIE PRODUCES IRRATIONAL THINKING.

The Webster's II New Riverside Dictionary defines the word "irrational" as *"not capable of reasoning, having lost mental clarity, illogical."* That's exactly the behavior that comes out of an ungodly soul tie. The ones who are bound by this relationship begin doing things that make no sense. It seems they have lost the mental capacity of common sense and reasoning. There's no way for another person to rationally understand why they do the things they do. The ungodly soul tie produces a lack of proper reasoning.

For example, there was once a woman whose soul was so tied to another man that she spent all of her income on him. The man didn't make as much money as she, so she paid off his bills, no matter how high they were, leaving nothing for herself. She was reduced to eating rice for weeks, because she had spent her income for his comfort. To her, that was all that mattered. She wanted to look good in his eyes, so it didn't matter to her how much she personally suffered. What is that? Irrational thinking. Lack of reasoning.

IRRATIONAL INTERPRETATION

A person that is entangled within an ungodly soul tie will even interpret the Bible to support their endeavors. Their mind has become so ensnared, they will even twist scripture to fit their misguided hopes.

Another example was a woman who so desired for her relationship to turn into marriage, that it was all she thought about. She became convinced it was God's will for the two of them to be romantically linked; she put aside all the warnings that she was out of order in her endeavor.

She was led by the Spirit of God to this verse in Psalm 127:1:

"Except the Lord build the house, they labour in vain that build it...."

God, by His Spirit of mercy, was trying to reason with her and help her to see that this relationship was not in His divine will. He intended for her to realize that she was heading for heartache, because this was not the relationship He had in mind for her. But instead, the woman interpreted the scripture to mean that God *was going to build* the relationship she had wanted between her and this man.

How could she erroneously interpret what the Spirit of God was trying to tell her? Irrational thinking. Not capable of reasoning. Her ungodly soul tie with this man had so con- sumed her thought life that it had now gained pre-eminence over the Word of God.

These people often are unable to accurately discern

whether something is spoken humanly or spiritually. People can approach a person and adamantly warn them against the ungodly soul tie. But the person entangled may not receive their counsel. Why? They are temporarily incapable of facing the truth because their soul is consumed, or bewitched. According to the doctrine of a person involved in an ungodly soul tie, everything they hear must fall into their imagined prerequisite of the way they want the relationship to be. Their soulish desire has led them out of order. Their spirit and body have no say in the matter.

THE IRRATIONAL PAST

Years ago I was working at a particular church. There was a husband and wife team who were both saved and working in the ministry of this church. They had small children who were all active in the church and serving God.

Out of the blue, this woman's old high school friends showed up at her door. They had decided to pay a visit to their old friend. The woman hadn't seen these people in years. None of them were married; none of them were serving God. Instead, her old high school buddies had spent their lives partying.

This woman accepted their invitation to dinner. Soon, she accepted other invitations to spend time with them, which escalated into too much time. Before long, these "friends" began sowing seeds into her mind about how much happier their lives must be since she had all this responsibility. Because she repeatedly heard their words, dwelt on them, and refused to end her relationship with these women, an ungodly soul tie was formed. All of a sudden, she started feeling different than she used to.

The woman began to despise her God-given responsibility. She decided that her husband was binding her, and she no longer felt like she loved him anymore. Her children became a weight to her, and she felt like she no longer wanted to take care of them.

Her "friends" would say to her, "You need to dump the whole bunch of them and come enjoy the night life with us. Be free."

By now, because of her constant association with these ungodly people, the woman's thinking became messed up. I want you to know that woman walked away from the ministry, left her husband and children, and moved out so she could run the streets with her high school girlfriends.

Irrational thinking. Not capable of reasoning. Totally illogical.

So I went to her and said, "What is wrong with you? Who has put a spell on you? You have a husband who is in the church and serving God, wonderful children who are being raised in the church, and a ministry to serve God. Who has put a spell on you to make you think it's okay to walk away from that?"

That was the theological part of my counsel to her. Then I had to come down the road and hit home.

I continued, "You need to go look in the mirror, because you act like you're going to get something better than what you've got! You ought to be happy someone wants you."

I am amazed by the number of people who have someone to love them, support them, and want to live their lives with them — and then some demonic thing is planted in their soul and suddenly they think they're Don Juan or some kind of hot mama and can get someone better. You had better hang on to what you have! You had better walk in the peace and blessings of God, thanking Him daily for favoring your life!

From the illustrations we've just discussed, you should now be able to spot irrational thinking. My motive was for you to see just *one* of the devastating potentials of an ungodly soul tie. All of these people knew their behavior was wrong. Some of them did these things secretly because they knew how unbalanced it was. It was only after deliverance that they were able to confess it and expose the works of the devil.

Somehow, these people all felt they *had* to act in this fashion *for themselves*. That's the personality of the ungodly soul. **Whenever the soul of a person rules their life, irrational thinking will follow**. These people were willing to give up the whole world for something that would never work out. Everyone could see it but them. Why? Because their entangled soul was in charge.

So far I've only used examples of women. But believe me, there are plenty of men that act the same way, and you probably know several. An ungodly soul tie entangles everyone in the same manner, male or female. Understand that the ungodly soul tie doesn't have a favorite gender.

BEHAVIORAL SIGN #2:

AN UNGODLY SOUL TIE CAUSES A PERSON TO EVALUATE THEMSELVES AND OTHERS ACCORDING TO A PREVIOUS CONTEXT.

Here's another example. Let's say a man and a woman are married. The man tells his wife that he's working late. She thinks he's working overtime. He's not working late. Instead, he has a girlfriend on the side and he's using this excuse to cover up the time he's spending with her. Tragically, their relationship ends in divorce.

The divorced woman tries to get her life together and serve God. Sometime later God gives her a godly husband.

Now her godly husband calls from work saying that he must work overtime. Since her husband is a godly man, he's telling her the truth.

But when the husband comes home, the wife is standing at the door with a frying pan in her hand. "Where have you been?" she growls. He says, "I've been working late!" Here come the accusations based on her past, "Don't lie to me!"

How many of you can see that the woman is "not here" in the present? She's having flashbacks. Because of a previous hurt and abuse, she is bringing the past into the now. But the problem is, she's not in the "now." She is living in yesterday.

There are people who are walking, talking and doing their daily routine, but the only thing in the present is their body. Their soul is still somewhere in the past. As a result, they judge everything that's happening according to a previous hurt or abuse from which they have not been freed. Their soul is totally entangled, so they doubt everything they hear.

The church is full of people like this. They were hurt ten years ago in a church someplace, so now they come to a church and judge everything by their pitiful past. That's called an ungodly soul tie and it needs to be broken.

"PAST" IS SPELLED G-O-N-E

The past is one of the greatest weapons against the mind and soul. God operates in the now and in the future; but the entangled soul operates from the fear and worry of the past.

We all face obstacles. They strengthen our "champion" nature. But to the entangled soul, it is easier to run away from an obstacle or quit, than to face more hurt and disappointment. The devil uses the past as a whip to keep you running. He has a tie, an ungodly soul tie, that has harnessed you to the failures of the past — and your damaged soul has allowed him to crack that whip on your mind at any trace of resemblance to the old situation.

When you live in the past, Satan will defeat you before

you get started. If someone has rejected you in the past, you automatically expect to be rejected again. You feel it's inevitable. Sometimes, you will even put yourself into a position or situation to be rejected. Something will happen and you will say, "Here we go again. I'm not going to try. I know how it will end. This has happened to me once and it won't happen again. I'm leaving so I won't get hurt." You are so busy guarding yourself from the past that you can't see your future. The past is over! The past is history.

Some of you have soulishly plowed the devil's field of torment and discouragement for so long, that you have dug yourself into a rut of fear and depression. That is why you are going nowhere. That's why it seems your life is standing still. You are in a soulish rut. And the sad thing is, in an ungodly soul tie to the past, you are the one holding the shovel.

PLOW THROUGH!

Jesus admonished us about living in the past. Look at Luke 9:62.

> *"...No man, having put his hand to the plough, and looking back, is fit for the kingdom of God."*

That verse doesn't mean that heaven has rejected you. It simply means that to push ahead, you must look ahead. If you look backwards into the past, you lose strength. Have you ever pushed a plow? It takes strength to push it. You must always look before you in order to keep the rows straight. If you ever turn to look behind you, you can't push the plow because your strength is weakened. It's not focused. When you look behind you, the rows you are plowing zig zag all over the field.

That's the way of ungodly soul ties that live in the

past. Their walk in life with God is up and down. They have no strength to look ahead and go for it. They are too busy using their soulish strength to protect themselves. They may be soaring, but suddenly a resemblance of the past comes and they're out in left field.

BEHAVIORAL SIGN #3:

AN UNGODLY SOUL TIE CAUSES A PERSON TO SHUT DOWN EMOTIONALLY.

Life will have its hurts, pain, and ups and downs. In fact, most of your plans will not happen like you have planned them. But that's no reason to jump off the walk of life and sit sidelined because of an unprosperous soul. That's why being spirit-led is so important. Being spirit-led guarantees righteousness, peace and joy in the middle of life's problems. But a soul out of order simply shuts down.

When a person shuts down emotionally, they are not in charge of their soul and emotions, nor are they able to give themselves to another person. If a past hurt or embarrassment has affected you that deeply, then your feelings and emotions are deadened. You cannot give what you do not have. If you are bound in your soul, you will always come up on the short end of the deal.

In the American culture, I keep hearing the same problem between husbands and wives. "They won't talk to me. They won't tell me how they feel. They won't tell me what's going on inside of them." And so the husband comes home from work, sits down in front of the television, grabs the newspaper and the remote — and sits there until he falls asleep. In the wee hours of the morning, he finally wakes up and stumbles into bed. When morning comes, he rises again to follow the same pattern.

Why does he do this? Because he's bound in his soul. He is afraid to feel anything or talk about anything, because he is trying to avoid more pain. You cannot release your soul to someone if you're not possessing your soul.

HOOKED ON A FEELING

There are also a lot of men left eating by themselves because their wives are running to the malls as "shopa-holics." There's something wrong. These are women who feel unresponsive to their families. Unresolved issues have caused them to shut down, and therefore, they respond to life in an unnatural manner. They are search-ing for a *feeling*, but they're looking in the wrong places. I've heard of people who will shop the malls all day, then see several movies, just trying to *feel* something again.

This is the case with many Christians who, upon hearing that we are not to live by feelings, falsely conclude that feel-ings must therefore be inherently evil. They then, in an attempt to achieve this unrealistic concept of spirituality, begin to deny all feelings and emotions. They soon become lifeless religious robots who say the right things, look right, act right, but feel nothing. They are now living in spiritual denial. They become cold, calculating and legalistic. They find it easier to *deal* with God contractually than to *relate* to Him personally.

However, very often when a person has hardened his soul to the point where his life seems empty and void of passion he may turn to strong secular music, illicit affairs, extravagant shopping, drugs or alcohol — all in an attempt to *feel* something that lets him know he is alive.

As I've just mentioned, if someone is searching for outside stimuli just to "feel" something, it's because they have unresolved issues running rampant in their lives. Usually, they are past hurts.

Sadly, this person has shut down his God-given feelings

and emotions, and turned to fleshly counterfeits to comfort and deliver him. Only now, problem upon problem has been added to his life because all he wanted to do was *"feel* something again."

If a past hurt has shut you down so hard that you are unable to communicate your feelings, become involved with another person, or show emotions, then you are still soulishly tied to whatever has hurt you. Sometimes the hurts come from a previous marriage, or a repeated sexual activity. In these cases, the people have never healed from their hurts, so they have allowed guilt, rejection, condemnation and fear to pad their soul. Who could feel or respond to anything with that kind of weight!

FANTASY

If someone has shut down his emotions, this person may begin to feed his soul with fantasy. The road of reality seems too hard for his emotions, so he enters the world of fantasy where everything turns out beautifully. He'll read kooky romance novels, become addicted to soap operas, or sit and dream away the hours.

Why would a person spend his or her life dreaming of fantasies? Because the outcome of a fantasy can be controlled by the imagination. Real life cannot. Fantasy will deceive you. That's why it's called fantasy. It's a myth or illusion. It is not real.

First Timothy 1:4, Paul warns us against the illusions of fantasy. Then he goes on to explain the godly way to handle our lives. Let's look at the *Amplified Version*:

> *"Nor to give importance to or occupying themselves with legends (fables, myths) [fantasy] and endless genealogies, which foster and promote useless speculations and questionings rather than acceptance in faith of God's administration*

***and the divine training that is in faith (in that
leaning of the entire human personality on God
in absolute trust and confidence).***

God makes it clear that He desires for you to deal with
the problem. Instead of finding artificial ways to pad
yourself, He wants your entire spirit, soul and body to
lean upon Him. That's what believing is. It's adhering to
Him like glue.

The situations of life call for complete dependence
upon God and His grace. He answers the cry of the meek
— those who believe and trust in Him — not the ones
who try to figure everything out by their own methods.

Don't artificially stimulate yourself with the
counterfeits. Fantasy and other delusions are not your
answer, because someday you'll snap out of their
mirage and find that life is passing you by.

HE'S THE REAL THING

Deception always incurs a misrepresentation, or in
other words, it abolishes the laws of truth and establishes
its own preferences. Deception causes you to drop out of
life. It causes you to be depleted of joy and peace. It will
constantly cause you to search for self-value. Deception
will even twist and contort a person's view of life until
that person thinks he doesn't want to live anymore.

If what I am saying seems foreign to you, that's wonderful. However, it is a sad reality to some of you reading this
book. These fleshly antidotes are steadily attempting to
replace the power of God in your life. Let's press toward
the real things of God, experience His power, know His
Word, and righteously live above the circumstances. God
has placed an abundance of love, leadership, wisdom and
direction inside of you. He has a beautiful, masterful plan
for your life. It's His desire for those treasures within you

to be released, so you can freely begin to give of yourself. Believe me, you will never regret the choice to abandon the works of deception and instead, to live for God.

BEHAVIORAL SIGN #4:

AN UNGODLY SOUL TIE PRODUCES AN UNHEALTHY, UNNATURAL DESIRE OR ATTRACTION TO PEOPLE, PLACES AND THINGS, EVEN TO A PERSON'S DETRIMENT.

That definition is long, so I encourage you to read it again. When an ungodly soul tie is binding you, it is the goal of the enemy to bring havoc in your life.

There are some who always gravitate toward, or are attracted to, people of the opposite sex who will hurt them. All of their relationships have been to their own detriment. Yet, somehow they manage to pick themselves up and head for the next inevitable heartache.

If your last five relationships have been with Bundy, Godzilla, Gomer, Baby Huey and the Tasmanian Devil, I want to ask you, what are you doing to attract such strange people? In the natural, you couldn't pick that many losers in a row, even if you tried to! It's unnatural to be attracted to every loser in town, or to be obsessed with a certain culture or lifestyle! However, this unnatural behavior is on the rise in our nation.

By the unholy influence of the devil, soul ties were created inside these people, causing them to be bound on the inside. The ungodly situations might have happened in their childhood, or even recently in relationships. Unfortunately, whenever they occurred, gaps were created in their souls.

"ALL I *NEED* IS LOVE..."

To simply explain, these people are *needy*. However,

that *need* inside of them is out of balance. They feel that they *need* to be the ones who make the difference in the adulterer's life; they *need* to be the peace for the violent abuser; they *need* to be the enabler to the alcoholic or drug addict. And with all their efforts, they'll find that it never works. Even by some remote coincidence, if the abuser did change temporarily, the needy person is left drained, broken and disillusioned. Why? Because the needy person gave out of an unresolved hurt, instead of giving from a spiritual overflow.

Instead of receiving the healing from the Lord, needy people constantly try to fix the problem themselves. Instead of allowing the Spirit of God to repair what is broken within themselves, they try to go back into a bad situation — sometimes with a different person — believing that this time the situation will turn out differently.

This is the case in which many people continue to put themselves into positions where rejection is imminent. Usually, this type of need is not asking for a handout. Instead, this type of person has an unnatural desire to feel important, to be needed or desired.

If you have spoken with these types of people, you will find that what I am about to say is true. These types of people want to accomplish some hopeless feat, not necessarily for the other person's benefit but so they can feel better about *themselves*. Unfortunately, needy people have a very low self-image, because they have never allowed God to heal them and establish them. Their self-esteem does not come from the Word of God or from the Spirit of the Lord. Instead, they have tried to "patch together" their self-esteem by works of their flesh. And so, through their fleshly quest, they end up in a deeper soulish circle of defeat, failure, and sometimes, even death.

You see, people who are really needy don't work on changing themselves. Instead, they will go through countless rejections until they find the one person who will accept them — usually a control freak.

ABUSES AND EXCUSES

For example, people get into relationships where they are hurt physically. Have you noticed that a physically abused person never talks about it? Why? Because they have placed themselves under the control of another person, and they don't want anyone to know that they are living in an unnatural lifestyle.

Sadly, a controlling spirit is surrounded by weak and insecure people. The controlling spirit has its regime with another unprosperous soul, because control has no power over the prosperous, self-authoritative soul!

It's amazing, but a person in an ungodly soul tie will usually remain with the abuser and suffer through the violent onslaughts of physical and verbal attacks. However, in their minds, they promise themselves, "If I can just live through this one, I'll pack my bags and leave. God help me to live through this one. I promise I'll leave." They may even go so far as to secretly purchase the plane ticket.

But then Mr. Perversion comes back home. In the usual demonic sequence, he begins his appeal, "Baby, I'm so sorry." Now, he cries. "I love you so much. I just lost control. I promise it won't ever happen again. I don't know how I would live without you." And on and on.

Did you know that almost every woman who finds herself in an abusive situation falls for that explanation?

She reasons within herself, "Well, the good times have outweighed the bad. I believe he's really trying. Materially, I have so much to lose. Could I even make it on my own? I feel sorry for him. I'll stay and pray that he changes." So she cancels her plane reservation and experiences the very same hell a few weeks later. If she's fortunate, she'll live through it.

NOW HEAR THIS!

There may have been good times. But it only takes one bad time to mar your life or end it. You may have many "material" reasons to stay. But what will they be worth if your life is tragically ended from abuse?

There have been a *few* domestic triumphs where both partners found true deliverance in Jesus Christ. But we can all think of domestic situations where the woman has not been fortunate enough to leave. She kept waiting for things to change. She believed the lie, and now we sadly shake our heads in her memory.

Unprosperous, needy souls lack self-determination, so they don't have the ability to say, "Hey! God did not create me to be beat up on and to be taken advantage of! God did not make me to be someone's verbal battering ram nor to be put under foot!" They do not seem to be able to follow through with the kind of strength that is necessary. They were already needy when they started in the relationship — now their self-esteem has been beaten out of them.

That is why, in Jesus' Name, we must follow through on their cries for help — no matter how small these cries are. We are commanded by God to release them from the hold of the devil and put the life of God back in them so they can be free from the domination and control of others.

Woman, pack your bags and leave! If you must do it secretly when the abuser is away, then do it secretly. God never intended for your body — His temple — to be abused. I don't care who you are or what your position is in life. You may even be a minister's wife and your abusive husband may be the pastor of a large church. If that's the case, then by all means leave before the entire ministry crumbles and you're left sitting in the shambles, condemning and blaming yourself.

I know you are hurting. I know it has been said that you are the problem and everything is your fault; but that's a lie. I know you are embarrassed and ashamed; but it's time for divine change. You may have been able to hide it from the people, but you cannot mock God.

Grasp your life and take it back! Go to a safe place where your spirit will be strengthened by godly counsel and prayer. If you will do that and submit to that, God will be able to secure your destiny and perform His will. But don't set yourself up with pre-planned ideas of what He is going to do. Just trust Him. He will never betray you or hurt you. He knows what to do in your life. God has abundance for you; but you have been searching for it in the midst of shattered dreams. Look up! Your redemption is as close as the air you breathe.

"BE MY HONEY AND GIVE ME MONEY"

Sometimes people get into relationships where they are hurt financially. In your group of friends, are you always the one that has to have the money?

You know, needy people get themselves into terrible situations. It seems they will do anything just to *feel* needed. Some people are not married and they move in with another person just so they can *feel* married. These people actually think they can counterfeit the covenant of marriage and get away with it. They want that other person so badly that they will break the hedge of spiritual protection around them and live a life of sin — all because their desires are unnatural. I'm here to uphold the Word of God and to tell you straight out — it will be detrimental to your life.

Here's one case of a needy person whose soul is out of order and ruling her life.

She's the one with the good job. She is the owner of the car and the one who signed the lease for the apartment. He's living at her house, driving her to work so he can run around in her car. She has never seen a ring from him because he's not thinking about marrying her. After all, by allowing him to move in with her, she's proven to him that a covenant of commitment is unnecessary. So the guy's got it made.

Then she comes out from work to find that he and his friends are in her car. They had fun while she was working. Her car is trashed because they all partied so hardy with it. Then she gets home and a party is going on in her apartment. They are eating all her groceries and none of them have a job.

These people are living off this woman and her hard work. They're taking advantage of her needy soul. How many times have we seen this in America? Someone works and then gives her paycheck to another person and provides them a rent-free place to live.

What should that woman do? She needs to move and not even tell those people where she went!

Ask yourself: Why is it that I am attracted to someone who is financially taking advantage of me? Friend, no one is so needy that she must support a derelict. It's an unnatural, ungodly soul tie. If you do not stop this unhealthy attraction, it will produce detriment in your life.

MISSIONARY DATING

Here's a prime example of an unnatural, unhealthy attraction to those that will cause you harm; the one who can never find a saved person to date.

Hear me: If you date unbelievers, they will be a hindrance to you spiritually.

Some of you are appalled at that statement. You're thinking, "Oh no, that's not true. I do what I call 'missionary dating.' If I don't date them, how are they going to get saved?"

Let me respond by asking, "How is that someone who does not love and serve your God feels so comfortable dating you? Are you that lukewarm? What is it that the two of you have in common?"

May I be blunt? If you are going to date someone, you had better have more in common than hormones.

Second Corinthians 6:14 exhorts us to use common sense and spiritual sense:

> *"Be ye not unequally yoked together with unbelievers: for what fellowship hath righteousness with unrighteousness? and what communion hath light with darkness?"*

Look at how the *Amplified Version* begins this same verse:

> *"Do not be unequally yoked with unbelievers [do not make mismated alliances with them or come under a different yoke with them, inconsistent with your faith]."*

Do you know what a "yoke" is? According to Websters II New Riverside Dictionary, a "yoke" is defined as *something that ties or connects; slavery, or bondage*. There's that word again — *tie*. And, it is interesting to note that when this word is used in reference to unbelievers, the definition infers *slavery* and *bondage*.

Jesus said that His yoke is wholesome, comfortable, gracious and pleasant; not hard, sharp, harsh or pressing. He even said that within that wholesome yoke, we would find relief, ease, refreshment, and recreation! (Matthew 11:29-30, *Amplified Version*.) The only stipulation with His yoke is that you "learn of" Him (verse 29). An unbeliever who chooses to remain the same will refuse to learn the things of God. There is no divine plan for a believer to be yoked with an unbeliever.

Why is that? Because one person is going down one

road and the other person is going down another road. There is no common integrity, no common bond, no common belief, no common lifestyle. One person is standing for the principles of God; the other for the principles of iniquity.

In days gone by, the farmers would strap yokes on the necks of their oxen. The yoke was a heavy, sculpted wooden bar with two U-shaped pieces that fit around the necks of the animals. The yoke forced these animals to couple together, work together, and carry the same load.

Imagine that example when you think of being yoked with an unbeliever. There's no way the two of you can couple together, work the situations of life together, and carry the same load. Light has no fellowship with darkness. In the natural, the minute light comes on the scene, darkness is dispelled.

A TORCH? A FLAME? OR A FLICKER?

Think of it this way. If you are fervent for God, the darkness in others should dissipate, not regroup, the moment you come on the scene. The unbeliever should have two choices when he is in your presence: he should change and turn to Jesus Christ, or leave. If darkness feels comfortable around you, then something is wrong with your light. It doesn't take months to figure that one out!

You need a fresh touch from the Spirit of God. God wants to re-ignite the flame of your spirit. He wants you to be overflowing and fervent for Him; unwilling to accept anything less than His best. He has it for you, but make sure you are in a church that is on fire for God — one that preaches on being "accountable" instead of "comfortable."

If you go to a "comfortable" church, you'll just find other lukewarm people to date. That's putrid to God. Lukewarm people are a mixture of the cold and the hot.

They are moved by belief, then swayed by unbelief. They trust one hour, then worry the rest of the week. They have just enough darkness in them to create a shadow instead of being a bright light.

There is a divine change that's coming to the Body of Christ. Make the determination to be a part of what God is doing. The secret to a fresh fire is in one word: *YIELD*. God will not overtake you, push Himself on you, or interfere with your will. You must yield and then He will come. Keep listening to that good Word, keep your heart tender and repentant, and constantly yield to the Spirit of God. If you will do that, He will divinely transform you. You will turn from a flicker to a flame; then you'll light the world by your presence.

BEHAVIORAL SIGN #5:

AN UNGODLY SOUL TIE WILL CAUSE A LACK OF JUDGMENT AND DISCERNMENT.

It is very obvious that a spirit of confusion comes upon those who are wrapped up in an ungodly soul tie. We have already discussed that they are unable to make proper decisions. Everyone else can see that their situation will not work out. Everyone can see that the soul-tied person is looking like a fool and is being taken advantage of. Everyone can see it — except the person in the soul tie.

A lack of judgment and discernment is very closely related to irrational thinking, but yet very different. With irrational thinking, the person does crazy things. It's almost as if they have temporarily lost a portion of their mental capabilities.

But with a lack of judgment and discernment, a person will react according to the distorted way he senses his situation.

Before a judgment can be made, one must interpret the issues at hand. Then the decision, or judgment, is made after considering those issues. Discernment is being *spiritually* aware of a situation — so we can already see the danger.

The ungodly soul tie tries to discern from the soul. Your soul is not equipped for discernment. Realistically, your soul cannot even make a judgment unless you've seasoned the soul and trained it by the Word of God. Even then, the soul can only make judgments based on the actual, written Word of God. Only the *spirit* of a person who is submitted to God can truly discern a situation and predict the outcome.

As we've stated before, when people are involved in ungodly soul ties they cannot see clearly because they've placed their souls in charge of their lives. They have taken the rule away from their inner man, or spirit, and signed over the title of decisions to their souls. In other words, these people are led by the senses instead of the spirit, so they will always base their judgment and discernment on *how they feel* instead of *what is real*.

As with other curses of the ungodly soul tie, they have lost their perception of reality. The ungodly soul tie is so motivated by its own desires that it overlooks the obvious. Can you see how this would set you up for confusion and heartache?

PERCEIVED NEED VS. REAL NEED

For example, let's say a man has reached his fifties. Instead of celebrating the life he's lived and looking forward to his future, he becomes depressed. He starts thinking about the days when he was younger, and how his life has since slipped away.

He reminisces about his old college football days and how popular he was. He looks in the mirror to see if he still has it — but now his chest hangs where his ribs used to show.

The man thinks and thinks and thinks about the youth he has lost. Not realizing that thoughts are seeds, the man continues planting discord within his members by yearning for the past. One day, those unrealistic "seed thoughts" take root in his soul and smother the warnings of his spirit.

Suddenly, this man decides he is going to regain his youth — at any cost. He begins to dress differently, act differently, and go to different places. One day he is out with his tight shirt and gold chains around his neck. A young girl begins to talk with him, and tell him how attractive he is. The man forgets that he's balding and his waist still measures 46 inches. He is overcome by his unnatural desire to be young and appealing once again. He begins to be willing to do anything for this young girl, because she feeds his delusion of a regained youth. It's an ungodly soul tie. He is suffering from a lack of judgment and discernment.

The man has deceived himself into thinking he must regain his youth to be worth anything. He has now lost all respect for the fifty-something years he has lived because of an undisciplined thought life. He has been deceived into desiring *what will never be* instead of receiving his marching orders from God for the next half of his life. He's trying to go backward while God is desiring to *anoint* him to go forward.

God has a plan for him within his age and his generation. But this man has willfully and sensually taken that plan into his own hands.

The man has developed an unprosperous soul because he's trying to live from the outside in. Remember, when your soul is prosperous, you live from the inside out, because your spirit is directing your life.

Don't you know that everyone can see how foolish he looks? Those who have never experienced the devastation that comes from an ungodly soul tie will laugh at the man. They will think he's suffering from a "mid-life crisis" and has gone off the deep end. But in reality, the man seeded his soul with wrong thoughts instead of the Word of God. Instead of seeking and hearing the plan of the Lord, this man thought he would be happier creating a plan of his own. He became consumed with his own thoughts and reasoning, and he became deceived. Now the devil has a foothold to destroy his life.

What has happened here? This man has been overcome by a *perceived* need, not a *real* need. It's interesting to note that Webster's II New Riverside Dictionary defines "perceive" like this: *to become aware of directly by the senses, especially to see or hear.*

We should all know this spiritual truth, that we cannot be ruled by our senses — our mind, will and emotions. That which we see or hear is temporary and can be deceiving.

ASK THE HOLY SPIRIT!

Did you ever stop to realize that true Christians are the *only* people on the face of the earth who have *God inside of them?* Think about that for just a moment. If you are a born-again Christian, you have God Himself living on the inside of you. He's there right now. You are the temple of the Holy Spirit — He is living in you and is readily available to counsel you, comfort you, teach you and guide you.

It's true — He's not living inside of the New Agers, or those who worship angels, or the Muslims, or those who say Jesus was only a prophet, or those who say they are a Christian because they live in America. The Holy Spirit lives in believers, the ones who have made Jesus Christ the Lord of their lives.

So let me ask you; if God Himself is living inside of you, why would you shut *Him* down and allow what *you* think, hear, and see to rule your life? How could our own limited, contorted counsel be better than the Holy Spirit's? How could we truly and permanently comfort ourselves? How could we ever be so deceived as to think our own guidance would bring lasting success? Can you teach the secrets of the universe? No, but the One who lives inside of you can. You'll never be a failure if you will listen to Him and rely on Him.

YOU ARE AS YOU DO

Now, just because we're focusing on the unbalanced, unprosperous soul, I do not want you to develop a fearful or warped concept of what I am saying and go off into extremism. There is a godly balance that we must understand, and I don't use the term "balance" as a spiritual catch phrase meaning "fear." To me, balance means strength, soundness and power. Balance comes from understanding the counsel of heaven. It is not reckless because it has supernatural power; nor is it swayed by the power of others.

There has been a warped, one-sided teaching going around in the Body of Christ. It comes from people who think they are super-spiritual, but are actually still babes in Christ. They are preaching that even if your body sins, you are blameless because your spirit is perfect and cannot sin.

It is true that your spirit is sinless, but the story doesn't end there. Did you know the Corinthian church had a similar problem? They had become so "spiritual" that nothing else mattered.

I have an announcement to make. It may shatter some of you, or be a heavy revelation to you, but here it is: *We are accountable for what our bodies do!* Doesn't your body respond when your name is called? Of course it does. Well, God marks your body down as *you!*

But don't just take my word for it. Let's settle this issue and read what First Thessalonians 5:23 says:

> *"...may your spirit and soul and body be preserved sound and complete [and found] blameless at the coming of our Lord Jesus Christ (the Messiah)."*

According to this scripture, we are held accountable

for our spirits, souls and bodies while we are here on earth. Once we have left the earth and entered heaven, we should have fulfilled our purpose here and entered into another part of the plan.

So you must understand that you've been given a body, soul and spirit, and you will answer for all three parts. Let's all thank God for the blood of Jesus!

Once you see it from God's perspective, the life of a true believer is continually exciting! There are new hurdles to jump, new challenges to overcome, and new situations to conquer. We can only control our bodies and souls, and strengthen our inner man by yielding to God, learning the ways of God, and relying on His Spirit.

Although there are many signs of an ungodly soul tie, we've only discussed a few of them. Now we have come to our last sign on how to mark an ungodly relationship.

BEHAVIORAL SIGN #6:

AN UNGODLY SOUL TIE PRODUCES THE INABILITY TO ESTABLISH AND MAINTAIN PROPER ADULT RELATIONSHIPS.

There are many people in America today who are adults physically, but they are children in their development. All of their relationships are overly gushy and glued together by some sticky, syrupy, soulish goop, sealed with comments like this: "Do you still love me? Circle yes or no."

Let's say you've decided to go out and eat with another friend and you didn't ask your syrupy friend. After you get home, there's a message on your answering machine. As you play back the recording, you hear this child-like voice on the other end: "Are you mad at me? I looked for you after church and then I saw you go off with Sister so and so, ...did I do something to upset you? Call me back."

It's what I call the "Circle yes or no" soulish mentality.

That kind of high maintenance relationship will wear you out! It takes too much energy to try to live your life being concerned about what someone else will think of it! Those people have failed to mature in their character. It seems that somehow they have dwarfed and stunted their emotions at age eight, because that is how they act! Just as a young child receives self-esteem or rejection from the central figure in their lives, so this "child in an adult body" acts the same way. These people will latch their immature souls onto you, and then think that every decision you make has something to do with them.

Don't be surprised where you will run into this kind of mentality. Some of these people pastor churches (though I might add, not successfully), some are on the mission field, some are in your families, some live next door, and some sit next to you in church. They all suffer from an ungodly, soulish problem—they're unable to establish and maintain proper adult relationships. They're never settled or secure. Instead— here's the uncontrolled soul—they are always trying to fix something by their own thoughts, plans or methods.

In the *Amplified Version* of First Corinthians 13:11, the Apostle Paul explains the situation like this:

> *"When I was a child, I talked like a child, I thought like a child, I reasoned like a child; now that I have become a man, I am done with child-ish ways and have put them aside."*

It's time for some folks to grow up and quit acting like children.

BE A REAL PARENT

Sir, here you are in your mid-thirties or early forties, and you're married. You have fathered three boys who live in your home, but you never see them because you still want to run with the "boys" and play ball. Instead of being at home, you have a whole list of things that are more important to you; and whether it's washing and detailing the car, or coaching a team with other boys, you are going to make sure these things get done.

Sir, the only boys you should be with are the ones who aren't seeing your face at home! Once again, allow me to be blunt — it's time for you to grow up and realize that being a father takes more than hormones. If you want to wash and detail the car, take the kids with you. If you want to coach a team, let your kids sit in the dug-out and be proud of their dad! Now here is the good news: It is not too late for you to grow up!

IS IT A TRAIN, A PLANE OR A SPEEDING BULLET?

NO! IT'S A SLUG

Let's look at the case of a man who is thirty-something years old and still living in the basement of his parents' home, trying to figure out what he wants to be when he grows up. This man has an old, beat up vehicle — and paid more for the stereo than he did for the car. And what is he doing? He is still cruising the high school! You would think if someone had a car that looked that bad, he wouldn't draw attention to it by playing his music so loud! Nevertheless, he plays it so loudly that the fenders rattle, because he chose to stay in a teen mentality after his body grew up.

Monday night he and the guys go out drinking. That's a high goal, isn't it? Tuesday night he and the guys play some ball. Wednesday night he's going to check out some cars. Thursday night he and the guys go cruising for girls. Friday night, they will all play pool. This man is thirty-something years old!

As long as the man remains in this pattern, he will never be able to establish and maintain proper adult relationships.

Sometimes a situation forces you to live at home. Perhaps your parents are elderly and are unable to take care of themselves, or their health is dangerously affected in some way, and there is no one else to see about them.

Or, perhaps you've been through a devastating situation and have lost everything. You've come back home to let God heal you and regroup your life so you can begin again. Thank God that you have a place to go. Those situations are perfectly understandable, because your ultimate goal is to fulfill God's plan for your life.

But when you are an adult and living at your parents' home because you have not matured enough to make an attempt to live on your own, there is a serious problem. Believe it or not, there are some immature adults who still live with their parents; never do their own laundry, clean up after themselves or cook their own meals; never buy groceries, pay bills or make house payments — because it would use up their freeloading gas money! It's true.

In the Name of Jesus, you must wake up and find the destiny for your life!

You were created as a human being in the God-kind of class, with a purpose for your life in the earth. He has made the gifts of heaven available to you. If you'll make Him the Lord of your life, He will unleash His power in you. The Holy Spirit will live inside of you where He will counsel, comfort, teach and guide you. All it takes is a step toward Him, and it's a step you must make. Afterward, the situations and circumstances of life will be surmountable.

You'll find a job and learn to budget your money. Soon, you will find your own place to live and become a responsible adult. There's a spirit-filled, fired up church in your community just waiting for you to become a part of their family. If you continue to trust Him, the goodness of God will come to you. Then finally, at thirty-something, you will begin to see what you have been missing out on!

THEY WORK HARD FOR THEIR MONEY — *AT WHAT?*

Let's look at another case of adolescent adults who are never able to establish or maintain proper relationships. What about at the office?

How many offices across our land are in constant turmoil because the office staff is like children. If you work hard and get ahead, they will get jealous. If you get a special idea for a project, they will try to submit it as their own idea, because they want the credit. If you are a whiz at your work, they'll try to find some way to trip you up. Instead of working hard, the childish, immature office workers would rather gossip and feud away their day. They're also the ones who complain that they're not being paid enough for what they do. Well, you would not have to pay me much to get rid of them!

Before I give another office illustration, understand that I'm not against humor or fun in the work place. I love humor! In fact, I enjoy laughing at myself instead of taking myself so seriously. We laugh and enjoy one another in our ministry office and in our services. I believe that laughter takes the edge off of situations and puts them into perspective. If we can laugh at ourselves, we can then deal with our mistakes and be successful. When a sound comes from a merry heart, it comes in the form of laughter.

Although I'm not writing this book on laughter, I've given you a few examples of laughter in the right context. But, what about the person who thinks life is "one huge joke?"

THE JOKE'S ON YOU

Here is another situation where a soul can become out of order. If this behavior is not kept in check, it can create ungodly mannerisms and the person will have trouble establishing or maintaining proper adult relationships.

While on their jobs, some are simply bored because

they have nothing to do. Their particular job may be based on one certain thing, and if that specific thing has not come in for the day, they're stuck. There is nothing else they can do, because as I've stated, their job is based on doing one certain thing.

Now, these employees are bored. That is when their minds turn idle and they begin to play. It's fine every now and then, as long as they entertain themselves and discipline themselves from making a lifestyle out of this behavior. But it is another thing if it begins to consume hours of their work day, *every day*. It also begins to have a different tune when it affects those who have other job duties and are working hard.

These employees now think it's "cute" to venture into an office and hide another employees stapler. Here's the other employee, rushing to meet a deadline — and she can't find her stapler. There is a client waiting who is also on a tight schedule. The employee turns frantic, trying to complete her assignment and keep this important client happy.

"Where's my stapler?" Another employee nods toward the jokesters. They are in the corner laughing and snickering.

Then, the pranksters go over to the copy machine and put the wrong color of paper in the machine. When someone rushes to the copier to make their copies, the wrong color of paper comes out. The pranksters jump out from a side office and laugh hysterically.

These pranksters think they are being viewed as popular, funny and entertaining. But in reality, they are seen as aggravating, immature and irresponsible. Because they failed to keep their idleness in check, they have developed an inability to maintain and establish proper adult relationships. Practical jokes have now become the center of their lives. Their behavior has turned foolish because their souls are out of balance.

THE SIEVE OF IDLENESS

Do not allow idleness to set your soul out of order. In the tenth chapter of Ecclesiastes, we read in verse eighteen:

"By much slothfulness the building decayeth; and through idleness of the hands the house droppeth through."

Don't lose control of your soul through slothfulness or idleness. Idleness is not a mental escape from life. Idleness will cause you to lose track of what God has given you to achieve. If you have free time on your job, then creatively spend that time in fellowship with the Lord. He will speak to you any place, at any time. He'll show you things to come and provide direction for your life. He'll share His secrets and wisdom with you. By evening, you will leave that job with a much greater spiritual understanding than you had when you arrived that morning.

No matter what your occupation in life, God has a wonderful plan for you. He not only speaks through His Word, but He's a God of demonstration as well. Let Him show you what He has planned.

Chapter 7

HOW SOUL TIES ARE FORMED

In previous chapters, we discussed the behavioral signs of an ungodly soul tie. From these outward manifestations, you should easily be able to detect if someone is having trouble in this area. If you see the signals of distress and the person wants your help, then you can explore the problem by finding out where the ungodly soul tie was formed.

We established that there are godly covenants; so we know that the ungodly soul tie is the counterfeit, or imitation of that godly covenant.

We have also learned that, to one degree or another, your soul was designed to be involved in every relationship. But in a counterfeit relationship, soulish bondage and unbalanced emotions will result. In the ungodly counterfeit, God is hindered from ruling your life because your soul has taken over.

There are natural relationships of the soul that are unavoidable, and sometimes, welcomed. God has created certain relationships for your soul to **be bonded with**; but never **in bondage to**.

Sometimes those natural relationships that involve the soul turn the wrong direction. Instead of the godly covenant they were created to be, they turn into an ungodly yoke of emotional guilt and bondage. It's important to keep your relationships healthy and your eyes on Jesus!

There may be more relationships that form naturally

with the soul, but we will only discuss six of these areas. I want to explore two principles within each area: first, we'll discuss God's plan for your soul within the relationship. Secondly, we'll look at what happens to your soul if the relationship takes an ungodly turn.

I encourage you to stay with me, now. Your freedom is rapidly approaching!

Chapter 8

How Soul Ties Are Formed

#1: ALL IN THE FAMILY

It is impossible to avoid it. When you were born into a family, your soul became naturally involved with them. God intends for you to have a godly covenant with the members of your family. He is a household God and He wants to be the God of *your* household! Joshua declared, *"...as for me and my house, we will serve the LORD"*(Joshua 24:15).

Now, when you were born into a family, there was a common bond established, a soulish cord that connected you. That is why you can be touched internally by what your family says, does, or thinks — even if they are not present, you can still feel it.

Here's what I mean. Strangers can say whatever they want to about you; but if momma says it, that's another story. It affects you differently. On the other hand, if the world is raging against you and it seems like everything possible has attacked you, a godly family can encourage you with just one remark. Just knowing they are praying for you will bring comfort. It is designed by God to be that way.

If we follow God's purpose, the family is designed to be a spiritual support to one another. Family members are divinely ordained to help one another fulfill their individual destinies. The way you learn to encourage and be a help-mate in your own marriage should come from the godly example set in your family.

A godly family accepts the responsibility of raising children for God. The family teaches the children how to pray correctly and instructs them in the principles of the Word. The members of the family demonstrate that God is a good God and that every choice has a consequence. In a godly family, the children have an understanding of the basic structures of life by the time they are grown. Even when these children make wrong choices, they are eventually able to recover themselves due to their upbringing and strong training in prayer.

I know one international minister who owes much of his foundational tenacity to his mother. At one time in his teenaged life, he wanted to compromise his character — just a little — like everyone else he knew in school. He started complaining. He began comparing his life to the other teenagers, asking his mother why she expected more from him than the other mothers did of their kids.

His mother snapped reality into him and, at the same time, zapped that illusion right out of him. She declared a truth that he never forgot. She said, "I don't compare you to the other kids your age. I compare you against your destiny in God." Today, he still uses that standard for his ministry.

GUILT AND MANIPULATION

Unfortunately, however, many families do not function in the way of helping one another to individually fulfill the plan of God. Instead, they are functioning detrimentally to one another.

Some families have never gotten on track with the plan God has for them. Instead of turning their family's loyalty toward God, they hold the family name over one another's head like a sledgehammer. Their loyalty becomes perverted and they begin to use guilt and manipulation to shame each other into doing what they want done. Thus, the soulish bond of the family becomes binding and limiting.

For example, some family members may want to buy you everything, then expect you to "owe" them in some emotional, serving way. They think that materialistic gifts mean love; but actually, it is a form of manipulation and control. They want you to be dependent upon them so you'll never leave their vicinity. If you try to leave, they'll curse you by saying "You'll starve to death," or "Your children won't have any clothes." What is that? It's an ungodly soul tie within a family.

There are many instances of the ungodly soul tie in a family, but here is one in particular. Let's say you want to make something of yourself and rise higher than you've been living. In an ungodly soul tie, the family resents you for trying. They will even rejoice if things do not go as quickly as you had hoped. They don't want you to have any more than they have. They exude an unspoken attitude of "We'll make you feel bad for wanting more than what we're doing. We'll make you feel something is wrong with you."

As long as you stay in the pig pen with them and agree with their particular outlook on life, everyone is happy. But when you make a stand against their pet doctrines, or when you say, "I'm going to climb out of this and do something else," they squawk! They'll go around muttering, "I guess you think you know it all and that you're better than the rest of your family. Just don't forget how we've helped you. Just don't forget how you used to act when you were a teenager." Well, I am sure this kind of family will not let you forget it.

This family does not want you to be happier than they are. They want you to stay like they are and continue to be miserable. They have enjoyed feeling superior to you, so they don't want you to do better than them. They begin to gossip about you and slander you — then write letters telling you not to be mad at them because they're your sister...or brother...and they *love* you.

So now you have decided that you are going to serve God. Already this type of family has you set up for failure. They think you're too harsh, too bold, or too this or that to ever be a "model" Christian. Of course, they have all been married six times, had affairs, lived for their jobs, drank and lived with the opposite sex — but they think they *know* what a Christian should be!

Quietly, almost secretly, they have set you up for failure. They begin to schedule every family get-together on Sunday — because they know you won't come and they'll have more to shake their heads and talk about.

Oh, but that doesn't stop them from making you feel guilty for not coming!

"How come you can't come with the family? Dad's hardly ever here. I suppose you have to go to church?"

Maybe you are spirit-filled, wanting to serve God with all of your heart. Perhaps you have even realized a call into the ministry!

Now you will really hear it: "I can't believe you're not going to be Catholic anymore! Our whole family came over from the old country, and we are all Catholic! How could there be anything more? You're turning into a heretic! Oh, I'm so ashamed! God have mercy on our family! Don't you know what it took for me to give birth to you? I was in labor for 143 hours! I almost died bringing you into this world and now you are not going to be Catholic!"

Here is the personality of a family with an ungodly soul tie: they will always cast you aside, or make you feel like the odd one if you dare to venture out from their personal perception of life. Soul ties... Guilt... Condemnation...All working through a spirit of control.

HERE IS WHAT TO DO

You should love your family and pray for them. **But you must not allow the actions and the attitudes of others to control your life**. Don't point fingers at their personal lives; just address the unjust slander that is aimed toward your life. It's okay to identify a problem, as long as you're committed to what you believe and you can communicate it properly.

You can honor your family and not lose an ounce of what you believe. To "honor" someone doesn't mean to turn wimpy and submit to what you know is wrong. No, to "honor" is to respect another person, but it is also remaining strong in personal integrity and stating the truth in the love of God. In fact, that is part of the meaning of the word "honor" - personal integrity.

You can say, "You can live how you want to live. I am going to love you; I'm going to pray for you, but this is what my life is all about. I'm going to serve God, be in the Spirit of God, be in the house of God, and worship Him. At family gatherings, if you want to see me, then do not schedule them on Sunday."

If your family chooses to live beneath what God has intended for them, then do not allow an ungodly soul tie to hold you down with them. Continue on with God and be what He wants you to be. If you stand firm and walk steady, your family will end up coming to you for counsel and prayer.

Remember, God is a *household* God. Claim your family for God, then leave the situation with Him. But whatever you do, see to it that you fulfill what God has for your life. It's never too late to start a new and godly generation!

Chapter 9

How Soul Ties Are Formed

#2: MARRIAGE AND THE "CLEAVERS"

I am not trying to be facetious, but there are some people who have no idea of what a true marriage is supposed to be. I've heard all sorts of thoughts about marriage: that it's an idea after high school, a joint income, a business contract, or what people should do legally to have sex and children. But if you have read the book up to this point, you know it must be more than that.

Marriage is a holy institution created by God between a man and a woman. With that in mind, we need to clarify two definitions here. A man is a *male*. A woman is a *female*. **Only** a *male* and a *female* can enter into a godly marriage. Understand that two females or two males cannot make a marriage. It never was, nor will it ever be God's plan for the same sex to live together in a marital relationship. In fact, He detests the very thought of it. In this day and age, we need to clarify some of our definitions to make sure that everyone understands what we mean.

Marriage is a *godly covenant* that was never intended to be broken. There are three decisions, or voices, that have agreed to this covenant — you, your mate, and God. It is godly because the three of you made a pact for this partnership. If one of you, or two of you wants to unscripturally break the covenant, the Third Person— God — must agree with you. And, He won't.

The marriage ceremony is a beautiful service with flowers, candles, and music. The dresses are attractive, the wedding cake is good, and the little flower girl is cute. But marriage is not about flowers, candles, music, beautiful dresses and cute flower girls. Marriage is about the godly covenant — and the entire Christian ceremony should focus around the vows of that covenant.

For those of you who think otherwise, reality has yet to hit you! A year or so later when all those bills start pouring in, those beautiful dresses and that cute little flower girl won't help you a bit. Be glad for the vows of a godly covenant, because that is where the strength of your marriage will come from!

In a godly marriage covenant, the couple has dedicated their lives to that marriage. The moment they speak their vows to one another, their spirits become united as one. God does not see me and my wife, Kathi, as two separate entities. Here on earth, He sees us as one spirit.

The godly marriage covenant also combines *all* your earthly possessions; not just what you list on a marriage contract. Today we symbolize that vow with a ring; but in biblical days, the couple cut their fingers leaving them scarred for life. They could not go into a place and take off their "rings," acting like they weren't married! It was almost impossible to hide that huge scar on the covenant finger!

If the ceremony includes communion, the couple is again vowing that they will lay down their lives for the marriage; and if necessary, even to the death to protect the covenant from being destroyed. As you can see, a godly marriage is nothing to play with. This godly covenant between a man and a woman is a very serious vow.

ANGELS LAUGH; DEVILS WEEP

Martin Luther once said, "With my wedding, I have made the angels laugh and the devils weep." When two strong believers join as one in marriage, it cripples the work of devils.

A godly marriage allows one another the freedom to be themselves; they don't play "the Holy Ghost" with each other. The wife doesn't compare her man to "Brother So and so." She realizes that "Brother So and so" was never there when times were tough, has never paid her bills, and never bought the groceries. In other words, her husband is the man that has blessed her. Her husband has set her free from worldly, fleshly debts. In a godly covenant, both partners have come to realize that "unconditional love" is the only debt they owe.

A godly man works hard and provides for his family. The wife does her agreed part in the family and "due benevolence" is enjoyed by both partners. The godly covenant is not religious — instead, they submit to *one another*; not to the man only. There's no harshness here; no abuse. There is no fear of the other's opinion; no one is a doormat. Both partners mature together in the things of life and in the things of God.

CLEAVERS AND RECEIVERS

Do you remember the old black and white 1950s-'60s television series called, "Leave it to Beaver?" That family was supposed to illustrate the ideal American family. And in some ways, they did!

There were no arguments in the family, no abuse, no illicit lifestyles. June, the mother, stayed at home, cooked fabulous meals, and always dressed like she was going to church. Ward, the father was extremely patient, diligent, and wise as he taught his sons, Wally and Beaver, the choices of life.

The boys, Wally and Beaver, could not do wrong without confessing it. They might try, but they would eventually confide in their parents, learn from their mistakes, and accept the consequences.

I liked their last name most of all — The "Cleavers."

Did you realize that is a key word in making your marriage godly? "Cleave." I didn't say, "deceive" or "peeve." After you join together in a godly covenant, God says the key word is "cleave."

Let's look in Genesis 2: 23-24.

> **"And Adam said, This is now bone of my bones, and flesh of my flesh: she shall be called Woman, because she was taken out of Man.**
> **"Therefore shall a man leave his father and his mother, and shall cleave unto his wife: and they shall be one flesh."**

To me, the word "cleave" means to be faithful to, adhere to, and believe in. When a man and a woman are joined together in a marriage covenant, they become one in the eyes of God. They are to believe in one another as they face life together. They are to be faithful to one another, raise their children together, and fulfill the plan of God together. Their union begins another branch on the family tree. It is a union, that together, will confront and conquer every situation throughout the years. It is the will of God for their marriage to continue in, or begin, a strong Christian legacy.

God never intended for you to be a doormat for your mate. "Cleave" doesn't mean totally helpless and dependent. God created you and your mate to be two different people, with different perspectives and different strengths. But, by His grace, He expects you to agree on spiritual matters and bring your opinions into agreement with the

Word of God. Marriage is a divine partnership.

APRON STRINGS

But, you have a problem in your house when your wife has to keep running home to Mama. You're in a bad situation if your mother-in-law is controlling your house. If either of those illustrations fit your condition, then there is an ungodly soul tie that must be broken. It needs to be confronted, with your mate, as well as analyzed, and ended. God's word concerning a covenant marriage needs to be strengthened in your household.

If you have trouble staying free from in-law interference, then move away from the problem. You should honor your parents; but no one has the right to interfere in what God has joined together, no matter who they are. God takes His covenant seriously; and anyone or anything that disturbs it will have to answer to Him.

DIVORCED, BUT MARRIED IN THE SOUL

Now I want to clarify another point. In a nation like ours, there is a tremendous onslaught against the families through a spirit of divorce. Many people were divorced before they were saved. Countless individuals have experienced tragic situations that caused a divorce.

There are legal, scriptural references to divorce. One is when the other partner is involved in repeated immorality; the other is when an unbelieving partner leaves on his or her own. I believe that it's also approved by God for partners to be separated if there are repeated abuse and significant danger to life. Remember, you are the temple of the Holy Spirit, and the steward over your body.

Now hear me when I tell you something.

Legally, you can be divorced from someone and still be soulically bound by that person. Why? Because when the two of you were married, you both became one in the spirit and joined in the soul. If your soulish involvement with this other person is not broken in the Name of Jesus, the other person will still have some kind of tentacle that reaches into your emotions.

I know of a case where a person had been divorced for ten years. This person never saw her "ex," nor did she have any connections with him. You would think that the smoldering emotions would have been gone by now.

But one day this person saw her "ex" on the street and the two stopped to talk awhile. That evening, the "ex" called this person on the phone and proceeded to tell her how "fat, dumpy and messed up" she looked — and that woman fretted and cried for several days! She went into a deep depression and battled a looming insecurity — all over the comments of a man she was married to ten years ago!

Are you battling with the same kind of soulish bondage? You haven't been married to that person for five years, and yet your "ex" can still say something that sends your whole week into a turmoil! Why do you still care what he or she thinks? Why is that still bothering you? I'll tell you. It's an ungodly soul tie, and it needs to be broken in the Name of Jesus!

You would be amazed at the number of people whose lives are so entangled and confused that even the courts ordered them away from one another! Those couples will fight each other in court, get their divorces granted — and then end up in bed together that night.

I don't live on the moon! So I'll give you another scenario.

Let's say a couple has been divorced. Since they have joint custody of the children, they still have to see each other and make contact. Well, one night the ex-wife comes over to drop off the kids at the ex-husband's house.

All of a sudden, this ex-wife begins to look pretty good to this ex-husband. There is something very familiar and comfortable about her, and he's liking it. He smiles at her in a certain way and makes loving gestures toward her. He begins to talk in that certain "I'll-take-care-of-everything" tone that used to comfort her.

The ex-wife starts feeling like she is back in the old days. Suddenly, she has forgotten all the bad times; she's just remembering the *good* old days. It's like she's been swooned away by subtle tones and gestures. Now, she finds herself hopelessly swayed by this sudden whirlwind of emotions. She can sense this little warm feeling in her heart and she allows it to consume her. And before you know it, the couple ends up in bed together.

Let's come back to earth.

That kind of thinking is totally illogical and irrational. By this behavior, the couple has proven that they are incapable of sane reasoning! What has happened to their minds? It is an ungodly soul tie.

You may have a legal document that says you are free from the marriage. But that legal piece of paper does nothing for your soul. Your soul may still be bound to the person, whether the state says you're free or not!

"TITLE SEARCH" YOUR SOUL!

When you purchase property, it's always wise to pay for a title search. The title search investigates all the legalities of a property, and advises you if there is a hidden lien, a second mortgage, or an encumbrance still owed against it.

If you don't contract a title search, you may buy some property and think you're the only owner of it; only to find out that someone else has a lien on it because of unpaid taxes or a second mortgage.

That is a good analogy for the ungodly soul tie to a previous marriage. If your soul is still bound to your "ex," then there is a hidden lien, or an encumbrance against your life. Unless you break that ungodly soul tie, you will pay the penalty for the rest of your life. You will never be able to bond into another relationship. The new person in your life will never be able to fully enjoy the privileges they are entitled to with "ownership" and commitment. Why? Because you can't give your life to another person *if it's still owned by someone else.*

You must settle up, forgive, and walk in the peace of God. Unforgiveness, bitterness, envy, and other such negative traits reinforce an ungodly soul tie to a previous marriage. Why? Because those carnal attitudes will hold you in the past. Those evil attitudes will keep you where the pain has happened.

You must let go of it completely — the pain, the resentment, the treachery — and go on with what God has for you. Your life is only crippled if you allow it. Before you can ever break the ungodly soul tie and be free, you must forgive the person that has caused all the treachery. Or, if that seems impossible right now, then forgive because you want to fulfill the Word of God. Forgive by faith, believing God will work in your heart and perform that attribute through you.

God has a future and a hope for you. Stop looking around, quit looking behind, and start looking ahead.

> *"Who shall bring any charge against God's elect [when it is] God Who justifies...Who shall come forward and accuse or impeach those whom God has chosen?...*
>
> *"Who is there to condemn [us]?...*
>
> *"Who shall ever separate us from Christ's love? Shall suffering and affliction and tribulation? Or calamity and distress? Or persecution or hunger or destitution or peril or sword?...*

"Yet amid all these things we are more than conquerors and gain a surpassing victory through Him Who loved us.

"For I am persuaded beyond doubt (am sure) that neither death nor life, nor angels nor princi-palities, nor things impending and threatening nor things to come, nor power,

"Nor height nor depth, nor anything else in all creation will be able to separate us from the love of God which is in Christ Jesus our Lord."
Romans 8: 33-35, 37-39 (Amplified Version)

Chapter 10

How Soul Ties Are Formed

#3: SEXUAL ACTIVITY

This chapter will be a real eye-opener to some of you. It goes without saying that in this day and age, illicit sexual activity is almost as common as paying a bill. However, in using that analogy, unlike the final payment of a debt, illicit sexual activity creates a debt that will never be satisfied.

Before I go any further, let's make sure we are following the same understanding. When I use the word "illicit," I am speaking of *any* sexual activity outside of marriage; or any perverse, distorted sexual activity between the same gender. The Word of God only honors the sexual activity between a man and a woman within a marriage.

I have noticed something that's interesting. If a person smokes, you can rarely tell it by looking at his physical appearance. If a person is a pathological liar, there are no signs of it on his appearance. If a person drinks, the signs do not physically show for many years.

But when a person becomes involved in illicit sexual activity, the results show up overnight! Immediately, the person begins to walk and carry himself or herself differently. The person begins to look at the opposite sex with a tease, and begins to dress in a lewd fashion. This person talks and even begins to laugh differently. Illicit sexual activity is a sin against the body, and it bears an instant effect.

It seems today that on a date, sexual activity is as normal as a goodnight hug or kiss. In the world, a couple is not "going out" unless they've slept together. I have even heard the confessions of some that they won't even date a person unless they have first had sexual relations with them.

I'm sure you've heard the deceptive cliché of, "I have to test the goods to see if I want the product." You might have even said it yourself. My friend, that statement borders on the stupid side of human mentality. It not only shows how ignorant and self-centered people can be, but it also spells out their destruction.

THE SEXUAL ROLLER COASTER

There are all kinds of weird opinions and man-made doctrines concerning sex. Some people think that sex should be shared with anyone, anywhere. To these people, sexual protection rates as high as brushing their teeth. They wouldn't leave home without it. According to their theology, a person is weird if he abstains from sex before marriage. We have the "free love" belief where degenerated married couples think they can have sex with other couples or other partners. So they host these "free love" parties where other married couples come to make friends and find intimate sexual partners.

Then there's the sexual activity between the same gender. In the Bible, Sodom was destroyed for this illicit behavior; and the fall of the Roman Empire was connected to its gluttonous, undisciplined behavior and its wild, homosexual orgies. Paul wrote in Romans that people who practiced homosexual activity were turned over to reprobate minds — yet the people who practice this illicit sexual activity want to "liberate America" by bringing it "out of the closet." Well, as a believer, I know what liberation is supposed to be, and this ungodly behavior won't bring it.

The devil uses illicit sexual activity to deceive, distort, and destroy the lives of millions. Understand that I am not against *the people* who make a practice of their destruction. I firmly stand with God *against the sin*, and I agree with God for His best to overtake every individual life.

Hear me in what I'm about to say. No matter how the government attempts to rewrite the laws or reinterpret the Constitution, there are no "rights" outside of the Word of God. Creating a governmental law doesn't free your soul or save your spirit.

HOLD ON! IT'S NOT JUST THE WORLD...

When it comes to illicit sexual activity, I'm not just speaking of the worldly disillusionment. Only God knows how many Christians are destructively involved as well.

Once there was even a popular, but very deceived, Christian leader who stated that all sexual activity — even within the marriage — was created as a curse because of Eve. This international preacher went on to say that multiplication was originally meant to happen the same way Adam was created — through the dust of the earth; but now mankind is cursed, so we have to have sex.

We don't have to debate how far off this man was from the truth. He influenced many by his erroneous teachings, until tragically, he died from a terrible accident. Unfortunately, that teaching still has followers today who curse women and exalt men.

Sadly, we have all heard the past problems of some tele-evangelists and television ministries. Churches have been destroyed because of the Pastors having adulterous affairs. But don't put everyone in the same basket. There are also *good* ministers' homes that wind up with their daughters pregnant or their sons in sexual trouble. I find it hard to believe that true Christians enjoy sowing havoc. Instead, I believe these tormented people are crying out for help, but they don't know where to find it.

Everyone is used to people in the world acting sexually neurotic; but everyone gasps when a Christian is found in trouble. How could a believer become entangled in illicit sexual activity? We are not talking about generational curses or undisciplined flesh, although those truths cause major sexual problems. We're talking about another issue: the ungodly soul tie.

If you choose to forget everything else you've read concerning sex, **make sure to remember what you're about to read**.

SEX: MAGNET OF THE SOUL

It was God who thought of the sexual activity between a married man and woman. It fits in with His kingdom inheritance He's given to us: righteousness, joy, and peace. The sexual relationship within a godly marriage brings great joy, peace and fulfillment. It symbolizes the marriage covenant of coming together — body, soul and spirit — and becoming as one.

Look at the *Amplified Version* of Hebrews 13:4.

"Let marriage be held in honor (esteemed worthy, precious, of great price, and especially dear) in all things. And thus let the marriage bed be undefiled (kept undishonored); for God will judge and punish the unchaste [all guilty of sexual vice] and adulterous."

So we can see from this verse that God takes very seriously His role as a witness to the marriage covenant.

We've just read that He'll judge and take vengeance on any area of a broken marriage covenant — specifically in the area of illicit sexual activity.

Sexual activity produces a soul tie. In a marriage, it's a godly connection with the soul. Outside of the marriage, it captures you into the whirlwind of an ungodly soul tie — and if you do not recover yourself and turn to God, you will toss and twist until you're destroyed.

In the *Amplified Version* of First Corinthians, chapter six, verses fifteen and sixteen, Paul describes the ungodly soul tie by illicit sex. He says,

> *"Do you not see and know that your bodies are members (bodily parts) of Christ (the Messiah)? Am I therefore to take the parts of Christ and make [them] parts of a prostitute? Never! Never!*
>
> *"Or do you not know and realize that when a man joins himself to a prostitute, he becomes one body with her? The two, it is written, shall become one flesh."*

I want you to read those verses again and think about them, because I'm about to present a very shocking reality. I want you to be ready to hear it and understand it.

Allow me to once again, be very blunt. Here's the key for this entire chapter. **When you enter into an illicit sexual act, a condom might protect you from disease; but it does not prevent the transference of spirits.**

In Genesis, chapter thirty-four, Jacob had a daughter whose name was Dinah. The Bible says that Shechem, the Hivite, saw Dinah, obviously lusted after her, and raped her. After Shechem committed this sexual act with Dinah, the Bible says that the *soul* of Shechem *cleaved* to the *soul* of Dinah. Let's read it, starting in verse one, and reading through verse three.

"And Dinah the daughter of Leah, which she bare unto Jacob, went out to see the daughters of the land.

"And when Shechem the son of Hamor the Hivite, prince of the country, saw her, he took her, and lay with her, and defiled her.

"And his soul clave unto Dinah the daughter of Jacob, and he loved the damsel, and spake kindly unto the damsel."

If you continue to read the chapter, you'll find that because of this illicit act and the ungodly soul tie it produced, that Shechem met with a destructive fate — he was killed by Dinah's godly brothers. **Illicit sexual activity will always produce destruction**. People have to face its destruction in various ways. For some, it produces an incurable disease that ends in death. For others, an unplanned pregnancy. With an unplanned pregnancy, we all know of the varied paths that these young girls choose. Still with others, illicit sexual activity produces a darkened claw of rejection, a low self-esteem, and possibly a criminal lifestyle. Only Jesus can set these people free.

You can see from those biblical illustrations that a soulish bondage, or cleaving, happens in a sexual relationship. If you have sex outside of marriage, you will receive what the other person is carrying spiritually and soulishly. That's why sex was only meant *inside* of the marriage, and why *outside* of marriage it is so dangerous and destructive. It's shallow to think that the only reason to abstain from sex is because you might get pregnant. That is just one of the devastating side effects and life-long hardships.

People swap demons by sexual activity. Do you doubt that? Okay, then let's explore your life for a little while, because God wants you to be free.

Let's say you've had sex with this person, that person,

this person, and that person — and now you are wondering why you can't shake the depression that's plaguing you. You are wondering why things are not working out for you, why you don't feel good anymore, where you lost your self esteem. You are wondering why you feel suicidal or why you just cannot seem to get the victory. It seems like you are so far down, unable to push through the heaviness. You're wondering why you have started lying and stealing, and doing crazy things that you've never done before.

I'll tell you why. Illicit sexual activity produces an ungodly soul tie. **When you lay down with someone, you get up with what they have**.

The Bible says that when two people have sex, they become one. The principle is the same, whether you entered into the sexual relationship as married or not.

If your partner suffers from depression, that depression became one with your soul. If a partner is plagued with lying and thievery, then lying and thievery became one with your soul. If a partner is tormented by demonic thoughts of suicide, those thoughts are now attached to your soul. If a partner is harassed and engulfed into the occult — that's right — those spirits are now latched onto your soul.

All of the junk that is wrapped up inside of that other person's soul, has now cleaved to your soul.

In a marriage, both partners keep their attitudes in check and their souls under godly control. They are "helpmeets" to each other, making sure their lives glorify God. In a godly marriage, it's all right for their souls to cleave to one another. If the couple is turned toward God, then He is blessing their relationship and their walk with Him.

But outside of the marriage, you have no say over the soul of another person. You are not that person's mate, and you have not entered into a godly marriage covenant with the person. That person is still free to act any way he wants to act, free to go anywhere he wants to go, watch anything he wants to watch, and take part in anything he chooses to take part in.

When God condemned sex outside of marriage, He wasn't trying to shackle you with "do's and don'ts." No! He was trying to give you life and life more abundantly! He knows what happens to two unruly or demonically influenced souls that attempt to become one *outside* of a godly marriage covenant.

But I have good news for you. You can be free from every demonic spirit that is attempting to torment you. Just keep reading.

Chapter 11

How Soul Ties Are Formed

#4: LISTENING TO VOICES

"There are, it may be, so many kinds of voices in the world, and none of them is without signification [or fails to convey a message] ."
First Corinthians 14:10

It is important for you to understand that the voice is the vehicle of the spirit. You impart what is in your spirit to another through the vehicle of your voice. When you sit under the influence of another or submit yourself to teachers, you receive much more than facts and figures. You begin to partake of their spirit.

Many people are being bound up in America today by psychics who use the telephone to ensnare their victims. Because of the "words" they receive and the friendly attitude in which it is conveyed, the listeners are unaware that they are becoming soul tied. Soon the spirit of confusion attaches itself to this directionless soul, until they are unable to make the simplest of life's decisions without consulting their own personal psychic friend.

Sometimes years later, through this kind of relationship, manifestations such as depression, listlessness, loss of ambition, financial ruin, and other disorders or calamities begin to control their lives.

The source—**soul tie.** The answer—**deliverance.**
In John 10:27, Jesus said,

"My sheep hear my voice, and I know them, and they follow me."
And in verse five of the same chapter,
"And a stranger will they not follow, but will flee from him: for they know not the voice of strangers."

There are some wrong "voices" that seem to be plastered all over our nation. If I see them on television, I simply say, "In Jesus' name, these words are bound and rendered powerless, and then I click right on past that channel.

If you listen to and receive the words from the wrong people, it produces a soul tie. Sometimes, I like to call this type of soul tie, "religious indoctrination," because "religion" acts the same way.

How does a person become religious? They have repeatedly listened to the wrong voices telling them things like, "the gifts of the Spirit have passed away with the last apostle;" or that "God doesn't heal." It's funny how entire congregations can skip over Acts, chapter 2, and it never hits them that thousands spoke in other tongues — but to them, "tongues are of the devil."

What is that? It is religious indoctrination; it is a soul tie to a denomination. It scares most of their members to dare to think opposite of their denomination. Religious people will not read the Bible to find out what is true. To them, if the ranking denominational figures said it, it must be so. Some are even so soul-tied to their denomination, they think that only themselves — or other like-denominational churches — will be the only ones in heaven! If you have placed a denomination over the Word of God, then you're snared by an ungodly soul tie.

YOU DO YOUR THING; I'LL DO MINE

There is a very strong cultural spirit in America that says, "Every voice needs to be listened to and evaluated." That is how our government has been. In their quest for equal rights, they have tried to force our nation into compromising the Word of God.

God says, "Every voice does **not** need to be listened to." Equal rights that are contrary to the principles of God does not mean justice, freedom and liberty for all. If a nation attempts to overthrow the principles of God, it will surely result in bondage, slavery and devastation.

The devil has no equal voice to God's. His methods and schemes have no equal grounds or equal time with the truths of God. Rights are not right when they compromise the truths of God. Anyone that repeatedly attempts to share an equal spotlight contrary to the life and ways of God, will surely pay a price.

I think our laid-back, "everything-goes" generation seems to have forgotten that God is still the God of the Bible. He is still the One Who split the Red Sea, the One Who opened the ground that swallowed Korah, the One Who sent the Flood. He's still the One Who walked on water, Who split the heavens and opened hell, plastering the devil and taking the keys of life and death. And He is the Only One that can save us from eternal death.

It seems that the world, and some of the Church, has a wrong definition for the goodness of God. To them, everyone can do their own thing, listen to whatever voice they choose to listen to, believe whatever they want to believe — and then they'll all "follow the light," go to heaven, and float around with beautiful angels.

Yes, God is very good. But His definition of the word "good" goes deeper than ours. A portion of God's goodness is the righteousness that judges evil. If evil attempts to harm the good, His judgment comes quickly and no man can hide. He gave His only Son to secure abundant life while on earth *and* eternal life after we leave earth. And if anything contrary to His Word tries to hurt that life, He steps in to take over. That's God's definition of "good."

LOYALTY OUT-OF-JOINT

There are many ministries, who, rather than leading people in true spirituality, will instead produce a dependent soulish congregation. Manipulation, guilt and obligation are tools that soulish ministries use to control their followers, rather than empower them.

How many Christians are soul tied into churches where they are not being fed or led in the Spirit, but they find themselves unable to move on to where God wants them to be? These kinds of soulish bondages refer to family, minister, or denomination — all of which needs to be broken before true spiritual growth can be addressed.

Have you ever wondered how false religions secured a congregation and followers? The followers were people who sat under demonic leaders and listened too long. These people developed a soul tie with the leader and received whatever the leader said. The leader twisted just enough of the right in with the wrong, and deceived the people.

The New Testament refers to these types of leaders as ones who preach doctrines of devils. These doctrines bewitch the minds of the people who receive them, and eventually, the people are no longer in charge of their own thoughts.

In a similar analogy, have you ever wondered why some people prefer to follow a totally charismatic personality over a person with character? It's called soulish tickling. The flash and stimulation of a charismatic personality tickles and delights their soul, so they follow it. The soul despises character, because godly character challenges the soul and harnesses it. It appears to be much more fun to act however you want to act, forgetting diligence, character and integrity. The Bible has a word for people like this:

"For [although] they hold a form of piety (true religion), they deny and reject and are strangers to the power of it [their conduct belies the genuineness of their profession]. Avoid [all] such people [turn away from them].

"For among them are those who worm their way into homes and captivate silly and weak-natured and spiritually dwarfed women, loaded down with [the burden of their] sins [and easily] swayed and led away by various evil desires and seductive impulses.

"[These weak women will listen to anybody who will teach them]; they are forever inquiring and getting information, but are never able to arrive at a recognition and knowledge of the Truth."

Second Timothy 3: 5-7, Amplified Version

Words are very powerful, especially if you receive them. The old nursery rhyme that says, "Sticks and stones may break my bones, but words will never hurt me" is a lie. If words are received, they begin to grow inside of you. If they are godly words, they will produce a godly fruit through your life. But if they're cursed and ungodly words and you do not dig them out from you by the truths in the Word of God, then they'll produce what was spoken to you.

The Bible never states that Samson had sex with Delilah. But it does say that he laid his head in her lap and he *listened to her voice* until she robbed him of his power.

My dear brother and sister, if you continue to listen to the wrong people long enough, soon you'll be just like them. You'll no longer be right with God. You'll start doubting what you once knew as a truth. Without a doubt, you'll lose your joy.

But listen to me — there is hope for you. Once again, your life can be right on track. Just keep reading, because I am almost ready to pray for you.

Chapter 12

How Soul Ties Are Formed

#5: IMPROPER ALLEGIANCES

Soul ties are formed through improper allegiances. That is to say, when we align ourselves with either the wrong people, or function with the wrong motivation, we become unduly influenced by the decisions and beliefs of others.

For example, we see in today's society an alarming number of young people who are being attracted to gangs. To these gangs young people give their allegiance. A gang, therefore, is nothing more than a network of soul ties. The identity of the individual is absorbed within the context of the group, producing a false sense of loyalty and security. Without individual identity and purpose, the members are set for detriment.

We see then that values and rational thoughts begin to change. Some young people who have family that loves them, actually begin to think this group of street urchins and thugs care more about them. And so it is, to their own demise, that to the gang they pledge their allegiance.

The need to belong, accompanied by a fatalistic mentality, produces a grim picture. The combination of this need and mentality thinks there is no future, so why try to be anything? Having no vision, they perish (Proverbs 29:18).

It is in these weaknesses that one is made vulnerable

for the ungodly bewitching of a soul. It is into the lives of struggling, disillusioned, and confused people that satan will send his workers. Thank God, through the anointing of deliverance, the burdens can be lifted and the yokes can be destroyed.

THE OX OR THE ASS?

Now let's talk about improper allegiances and going into business dealings with people.

There is a difference in doing business *with* and being *in* (or bound to someone) in business. When you sign your name on a contract with someone, you are bound by your word. Jesus taught to owe someone a debt meant you were not totally free, but rather a servant to the lender.

There are times, of course, when it is wisdom and more profitable to borrow money. An example would be to acquire equity or letting money work for you toward a greater end. However, there are a great number of people who glibly sign their name or go into business with people and find that peace and joy have left them. Now they are frustrated, anxious, stressed out, *and* soul tied.

Look at the warning of Deuteronomy 22:10.

> *"Thou shalt not plow with an ass and an ox together."*

If you wanted to plow a field, you could use either the ox or the ass — but not together! The ox is a servant with a sacrificial nature. And the ass has a rebellious, headstrong and stubborn nature. They may both plow the field; but their methods are vastly different.

How many people align themselves to someone who is unyielding and demanding, while they find themselves in the perpetual position of giving, serving and doing all the work?

> *"Be not one of those who strike hands or of those who are sureties [co-signers] for debts. If thou hast nothing to pay, why should he take away thy bed from under thee?"*
>
> **Proverbs 22:26, 27**

Before you go into business, or sign on the dotted line, make sure there are no strings — both seen and unseen — that you do not want attached !

SOUL TRAPS ON THE JOB

To further investigate this point, we see that some people are soul-tied to their jobs.

Remember, you can do business *with* people and work for people, or have people work *for* you without allowing yourself to be bound.

Some folks, though, spend all their hours at home griping and complaining about "Jerry" on the job. When they arrive home from work, the family has to endure the daily "Jerry" report.

"Jerry" is more in charge of how you feel and what kind of a day you have, than you are. "Jerry" is no longer a person on the outside. He has been used to getting "under your skin," or more accurately, inside of your soul. He is now the physical embodiment of all the things you hate. It seems you cannot leave him at work. He is *always* with you.

Again, you must learn how to work around other people without allowing them to affect your soul.

"WITH HIM THOU SHALT NOT GO!"

Proverbs 22:24, 25 forewarns us of wrong relationships and the consequences they'll produce in our lives.

"Make no friendship with an angry man, and with a furious man thou shalt not go, lest thou learn his ways and get a snare to thy soul."

Church problems, schisms, and splits are caused by angry people. Generally, they find someone to go with them. They recite their grievances and issues over and over until they soul tie those who listen to their poison.

Godly authority must correct the rebellious. If the rebellious ones react in anger, they may leave the ministry. What is interesting, however, are the snared souls who often times will go with them. Somehow, now their relationship to the pastor has been changed by their friendship with the angry man.

The Bible is clear, **"with him thou shalt not go."** The end result is, you will learn his ways and it will become a snare to your own soul.

There are illegitimate churches whose foundation is not a divine mandate, but rather a disagreement they had elsewhere. They are rebellious and uncovered.

The only ones who follow them are bewitched and are wasting years off of their destinies, deceived into thinking great things are in store for them.

Sometimes, there are those who come to join my church by the fact that they are angry with someone else. I do not receive members like that into my church. I will not allow them to snare my soul.

You need to realize that, like a lethal snake, soul ties have a hypnotic effect. The goal is to bring people into a lethargic state so they may be devoured. If you do not let go and get free, you will become easy prey.

Chapter 13

How Soul Ties Are Formed

#6: IDOLIZATION

Before we start this chapter, I want you to understand that I'm not speaking of proper role models or proper authority. Instead, I am going to address a problem in our nation, because the American culture loves idolization.

In the *Amplified Version* of Acts, chapter eight, verses nine through eleven, we can read about the effects of idolization.

> *"But there was a man named Simon, who had formerly practiced magic arts in the city to the utter amazement of the Samaritan nation, claiming that he himself was an extraordinary and distinguished person.*
>
> *"They all paid earnest attention to him, from the least to the greatest, saying, This man is that exhibition of the power of God which is called great (intense).*
>
> *"And they were attentive and made much of him, because for a long time he had amazed and bewildered and dazzled them with his skill in magic arts."*

The people of Samaria had allowed this ungodly

person to become an idol in their community. If you read those verses carefully, you will notice that through their idolization of Simon, he had bewitched them.

Remember, in the beginning of this book we discussed that the bewitching of your soul, or the spell on your soul, is always caused by a "who," not a "what." The same is true for idols. When you idolize another person, you are looking to another to fill the voids in your own life.

Anything that you embrace above God is an idol. God is the only One that should influence the course of your life. Therefore, if you embrace an idol you have opened the door for ungodliness to influence your course.

THE DECEIT OF PORNOGRAPHY

Pornography is a form of idolization; and unfortunately many men and women are held captive to it. They look at a woman or man on the page of a magazine, on the screen, on a poster, and they begin to idolize and fantasize about them until their emotions become drastically affected. They can no longer think properly.

At first, they started with just a little porno. Now, they've seared their consciences with the "little," so they crave more and more perversion. The more it stimulates them, the better it is; so they stop at nothing. Now they see every woman or every man as a sexual object. Every conversation has an innuendo. They even begin to dress differently. Some have become so desensitized, they'll even go as far as child pornography. It has also been professionally documented that the stimulation of murder is directly linked to pornography. What is it? It started as a fantasy, and ended as a devastating, ungodly soul tie.

IS ELVIS DEAD?

We make idols out of movie stars, sports figures, or whatever else comes out of Hollywood, Nashville, or Motown. When you begin to thrust your fantasies upon these idols, you have allowed them to have an unnatural ability to bind and control your life; even though you've never met them.

Have you ever heard of people turning their entire homes into Marilyn Monroe theaters, complete with wall-to-wall memorabilia? Then, they spend their savings to take a trip to her grave vault, where they can buy more memorabilia and wallpaper their home.

You may say, "Oh, they're just enjoying themselves. That's their hobby."

That is not a hobby! That's a consuming, soul-tying, fanatical fantasy! These people aren't living in the real world. They're living in the '50s, thinking that they know Marilyn personally! They've made her an idol, and their souls are tied to a person who has been dead for years.

Did you know there are still people in America today who make varying decisions based on where Elvis was sighted? It's true! Someone needs to tell these people that Elvis has not been spotted at Wal Mart. He is not on a UFO, and he is not living on an island in the South Pacific hiding from the underworld. Elvis is dead. It is over for him. But yet, we still see these men running around, letting their sideburns grow, trying to talk like Elvis.

Is your soul tied to a man who has been dead since 1977? We make such idols out of people, that we even try to look like them. Who **are** you, anyway?

We all remember the Beatles. If you don't remember them, I'm sure you've seen their comeback attempt through videos and CD's. In the 60's, whenever The Beatles hit the stage, or showed up in a city, the young people would shake and vibrate. The television showed people passing out, or having to get fanned. Do you remember seeing the girls screaming, crying and wildly fighting to touch Paul, George, John or Ringo? Even when their movies came out, it was said that girls screamed and cried when the faces of The Beatles came on the screen!

What was that? That was a demonic, ungodly soul tie. These young people had sat for hours, dreaming at pictures, listening to their music and fantasizing about them until the Beatles became their idols. When they actually saw "The Fab Four" in person, they went into the manifestation of what their soul had created within them.

Here's an example that's more to date. When Michael Jackson fled to Singapore several years ago, people gathered outside of his hotel. When they saw his glove — *only his glove* — in the window, they fell over, weak and fainting.

What was that? That was another demonic, ungodly soul tie. These people were so consumed with Michael Jackson, that he was all they thought about and lived for. And they did not even know him.

LIFESTYLES OF THE RICH AND FAMOUS

What about the soap operas? Here we go! It was fine for me to talk about Marilyn, Michael, and Elvis, but you don't want me to touch your soap operas! Well, just hang on and keep reading. Your help is about to come.

Soap operas are designed to be a soulish trap. Each day the show introduces a new cliff hanger, or a new diabolical plot. People have shared with me that soap operas are so addictive, it only takes two or three days to get hooked. The sad thing is, people get so wrapped up in these soap operas, that they begin to idolize the characters on the shows! As a result, they're not happy with their own lives anymore.

I remember when everyone was watching "Dallas." In

fact, the show was so popular that you didn't have to watch it because everyone talked about it! You could always hear what was happening.

The show revolved around this mythical Texas family in the oil business. There was the mean, slick and filthy rich J. R. Ewing. He would jet from place to place, and sit from one plush chair to another as he made those crooked business deals. Iit seemed like America stopped cold the night J. R. was shot. Everyone was at their television sets to see who shot J. R.!

The other members of the Ewing family would also jet around from place to place, just to have lunch somewhere different. They didn't have jobs like you and I.

Let's say this middle-class woman was a faithful fan of "Dallas." After she watched the Ewings for awhile, it made her painfully aware of her meager surroundings. She started noticing that J. R. looked pretty nice. In fact, she thought that it might be nice to have a man like that. He was always dressed in his best from head to toe. She figured that he must smell good; and even his nails are clean, white and trimmed. And think of all that money; all that luxury; all those clothes — and suddenly, the show ended.

The woman looks over at her hard-working mechanic husband, as he sits in his chair, snoring — complete with the musty smell of motor oil and black grease still under his finger nails.

Now, her man is a good provider, a good husband, and a good father. He loves his family. But, the woman begins to feel cheated and restless. Why? She has allowed a mythical fantasy to bewitch her. Now, this woman trudges through the week until the next shining episode comes on. Do you see how she's setting herself up for heartache?

Some people get so emotionally attached to these fictitious characters, that they cannot bear to miss a show. If they are not at home to watch it, they will set their VCR's and tape that segment. Everything in their lives stops when this television show comes on.

Some people have their souls so tied to these characters, that you could be talking to them for fifteen minutes before you realize they're talking about a made-up person!

It happened to me once. A person came up to me and said, "Pastor, we've got to pray." I said, "What's the matter?"

"Suzy's going to have surgery."

"Suzy? Well, do you want us to come into agreement with you and pray about it?"

I talked with this person for several minutes before I found out that "Suzy" was a character on "General Hospital"! I am telling you, this person was hurting over this surgery! I have even heard of people coming to church, and crying over something like Antwoine on "As The World Turns" getting a divorce!

I know it sounds funny. But gradually, *if you don't change* what is happening to you, these *shows will begin to change* your realistic view of life.

I realize that some of you watch these shows in a desperate attempt to escape from your painful life. I want you to be free in the Name of Jesus.

But then there are some of you that watch these shows because you're just plain lazy! You are sitting there with laundry piled up to the ceiling, and you're watching someone else on the "Lifestyles of the Rich and Famous," wondering why you cannot get anywhere in life.

You need to shut off the television, and come out of the dream world. Get out your box of detergent, and put some diligence into your life! Then, your surroundings will change. Remember, the prosperous life starts from the inside and spreads to the outside.

Jesus wants you to be a whole person; not fragmented in one area, and torn in another. He wants you to experience the pleasure of wholeness. Are you ready? Then let's continue.

Chapter 14

THE ANSWER

If you have read this entire book, you should now be aware of the differences between a godly relationship and an ungodly soul tie. I don't think that it's important to reiterate what has been said. If you fit into any of the categories we have discussed, then it is time for the answers.

There are three steps that must take place before an ungodly soul tie can be broken. We will briefly discuss these areas; then I will pray for you.

1: YOU MUST WANT TO BE FREE

First, you must have a desperate desire to be free from any ungodly, soulish activity. A desperate mentality will always bring answers. God has given you a will, and He respects it. The Holy Spirit also respects your will. He will never push Himself upon you; and He will not force you to accept spiritual and soulish freedom, if you don't want it. He'll allow you to live in misery if you choose to.

Yielding is the key to receiving from God. Yielding comes when you want God to intervene in your life. When your awareness rises to the place where you realize that you need something from God, **that is when you yield**. Relax in Him, and do not wait for lightning bolts.

Once you yield to the Spirit of God, He will teach you and show you much more than I've been able to share in this book. Why? Because yielding to God brings peace.

Before you yielded to Him, your life was filled with anxiety and constant turmoil. You refused to submit to God because you wanted things to happen in your own way. The answers from God always come when you rest in Him. When you are in peace, God will speak to you.

So, before we go any further, if you want to be free from ungodly soul ties, then begin right now to yield yourself to the Spirit of God. Tell Him that you no longer choose to live your own way. Tell Him how much you love Him and how much you trust Him.

Let His Spirit go into the deep parts of your being, and allow Him to deal with the issues of your heart. Believe that God is doing something in you, because if you're desperate He's working!

2: LET GO

After you have yielded to God, He will require you to let go of the ungodly soul tie. The real issue here is "trust." At first, you may even be fearful to let go. You may not understand how everything is going to work. You may be afraid of the pain your soul might feel. I'll be honest with you. Your soul will feel pain because it is no longer getting its way. In fact, your soul may scream so loudly that you'll wonder if you will ever be normal again. You cannot trust your soul. **But you can trust Him.**

God knows your future, and He knows how to get you where you need to be. God also knows your heart, your desires, and your needs better than you know them. You may think you know yourself — but He knows you far better than you know yourself. He knows the real desires of your heart. The ungodly soul tie puts so many different masks over your heart, that you'll be surprised to see what God will show you about yourself. But you must let go of what you have been holding onto.

There's a very interesting story that I feel illustrates

the principle of letting go. The story is a true one.

In Africa, some of the native tribes feast on chimpanzees as a regular part of their diet. Killing a monkey in Africa is no different than killing a cow in America. Food is the primary reason for the kill.

For many months, the tribe couldn't figure out how to catch the chimps. They would set the traps, and place bait just inside the door. But the chimps were too quick. They would run by, snag the bait, and be gone before the trap door shut.

Then the tribe tried to place the bait in the middle of the trap. They thought by the time the chimp got to the middle, the trap door would close. But every time they came to the traps, the bait was gone and no chimp was found. Somehow, the chimpanzees had discovered how to run into the trap, get the bait, and still be gone before the trap shut. It seemed they were just too smart and too quick for the tribe.

The tribe tried every method they knew; but all had failed. Then, someone had a brilliant idea. It was a long shot; but the man noticed a weakness in the chimps.

They built the trap the same as before. Except this time, they hid the bait in a box that had been bolted into the ground. Through an opening just large enough for the chimp to get his hand through, the bait would glisten. The secret was this: the opening of the box was too small for the chimp to pull both his hand *and* the bait out at the same time. He would have to let go of the bait to get away.

Sure enough, the trap worked. The chimps would venture into the trap to check out the box. Once they saw the bait, they'd reach their hands down into that box to grasp it. They wanted the bait so badly that they refused to let go of it, even though the box refused to budge. So, the tribe walked right in with their clubs and easily killed the chimps — with their hands still in the box.

It was amazing that the chimps, who were so smart

and so quick, could be beaten so easily. The answer was really simple. All the chimpanzees had to do was *let go* of the bait, and they could have run free.

The same is true for the ungodly soul tie. The only way you can be defeated is if you refuse to let go. Trust me, the box is bolted into the ground. There is no other way out. You can't take the bait and run free. You must let go of the ungodly soul tie and walk away from it. Outside of your "box" is where the blessings are.

#3: YOU MUST REPENT

This is not the "turn or burn" section; this is the "life and freedom" section! In order for the ungodly soul tie to be broken, you must acknowledge a few things before the Lord.

First, it is important to realize and understand that with an ungodly soul tie, you have neglected the Spirit of God. In an ungodly relationship, you have allowed your soul to rule your life. By doing so, the will of God and the plan of God was temporarily aborted in your life.

Instead of relying on the Spirit of God, you have depended upon sense and reason to lead you and make the decisions of your life. You might have even misinterpreted the Word of God to satisfy your need. Often, sinful choices turn into regularized behavior, and those choices need to be confessed to the Lord.

The *Amplified Version* of Romans, chapter eight, verse six, describes the process in detail:

> *"Now the mind of the flesh [which is sense and reason without the Holy Spirit] is death [death that comprises all the miseries arising from sin, both here and hereafter]. But the mind of the [Holy] Spirit is life and [soul] peace [both now and forever]."*

Notice that Paul says the mind of the flesh is sense and reason without the Holy Spirit. The mind of the flesh, or the rule of the soul, always leads to destruction and death. Your soul was never designed to make the decisions for your life; therefore the soul is not equipped to bring you life.

But look at the next part. Paul goes on to say that the mind of the Spirit is both life and soul peace. When your spirit is in control and making the decisions for your life, it brings your soul into peace. Your spirit is equipped with everything you will ever need. Your spirit should rule your thoughts, your emotions, and your body. When the spirit is in control, you will hear from God and know exactly what to do.

If you have understood what I've shared, then it is important to repent from forming the ungodly soul tie and becoming involved with it. By forming an ungodly soul tie, both the plan of God and the voice of your spirit were over-ruled by the plan of your soul.

God is a loving God. He is very tender with those who have sinned and have come to Him for forgiveness. He is not concerned about those who miss it, because we all miss it from time to time. He is concerned about those who miss it and refuse to repent. He's concerned about those who miss it, then sweep it under the table and try to go on with their lives. It doesn't work that way.

Once repentance has come, you'll find that you have recovered much more than you have lost. That is the New Testament, or new covenant principle that Jesus came to fulfill. Hear as He announced,

"The Spirit of the Lord [is] upon Me, because He has anointed Me...to preach the good news...to the poor; He has sent Me to announce release to the captives and recovery of sight to the blind, to send forth as delivered those who are oppressed [who are downtrodden, bruised, crushed, and broken down by calamity],

*"To proclaim the accepted and acceptable
year of the Lord [the day when salvation and the
free favors of God profusely abound]."*
                    Luke 4:18-19, Amplified Version

My friend, today is your day.

Now, let's stand before the throne of God. He will
hear us as we pray. First, pray your own personal prayer
of repentance to the Lord. Be free to tell Him whatever
you need to tell Him.

After you have prayed your own prayer, receive His
forgiveness and strength.

Now, place your hand on your body, and say this
prayer out loud as I pray it for you.

**"Father, in the Name of Jesus, I come against
every hindrance, every hurt, every abuse, every
attack, every ungodly allegiance in this life, every
ungodly voice, and every ungodly idol that has
placed itself on the throne.**

**"I break every evil word that has been spoken
against this life in the Name of Jesus. I curse the
ungodly heritage and say that in the Name of
Jesus, a new and godly generation shall begin this
very day.**

**"By the authority of Jesus, I cancel the effects of
every threat, every lie, and every deceit that has
been placed against this life. I reverse the curse, and
speak that righteousness, joy and peace shall abundantly reign in its place.**

**"And God, as Your servant, I ask you to restore
what the enemy has stolen from this life, and I ask**

You to fill any void in this life according to Your plan and destiny.

"I say that in the Name of Jesus, every nervous condition and every fear is now gone; every suicidal thought is destroyed; and by the Blood of Jesus Christ, I tear down and reverse the effects of every tormenting, harassing spirit in this life.

"Father, thank You for this precious life that is praying this prayer with me. Thank You for causing them to live in this generation. Thank You for the destiny that is planned for them. And thank You Father, for speaking to them, and showing them the things to come. We thank You for the grace, the power, and the anointing of the Holy Spirit that causes us to succeed.

"We love you, Father. In Jesus' Name, I thank You for this new day of freedom."

Continue to thank God for what He's doing in you. The grace of God is a miracle, and that grace has come upon you.

You'll begin to see things differently now. It's time to strengthen your spirit with the Word of God. **The stronger your spirit, the clearer your focus.**

It may seem like it's been awhile, but life is going to be new and exciting for you. The more thankful you become for the grace of God, the more He will strengthen your life with it.

Now, take that strength and the freedom you have been given, and be counted among the believers in Acts 17:6 who "turned the world upside down" for the kingdom of God!

Notes

Notes

Notes